1

Clean Comfort:
An Adventure in Food, Courage, and Healing: How I Went From 345 Lbs. to A Size 8 Without Dieting, Surgery, or Losing My Sanity

By Stacey Morris

Dedication

First and foremost, this book is dedicated to anyone ever caught in the cycle of despair known as dieting and binge-eating. Only those who've walked this road know the frustration, self-recrimination, and shame that comes from ping-ponging back and forth between the two extremes. This book is for you...I share my experience, long-term results, and hope (as well as recipes) with you so you know there is indeed a way out. Motivation is the wild card, though, and it kicks in only when you're ready. That's how it happened for me and dozens of people I've met through Team DDPYOGA.

And to **Diamond Dallas Page**, creator of DDPYOGA and **Terri Lange**, Godmother of DDPYOGA, how can I put thanks to you in a single sentence? Both amazing examples of reinvention and being jaw-droppingly fit at any age, you guided, mentored, and cheered me on during my 18-month journey of shedding the physical burden of excess weight and taught me what it takes to *keep* it off. You had the answers that diets du jour and celebrity fitness books did not. And you wanted nothing in return other than to see me succeed. Thank You with all my Heart for caring and for taking the time out of your own busy lives. As you know, my Life has blossomed in ways I never thought possible.

A Massive Thank You to Team DDPYOGA member and all-around technical wizard **Robert McLearren** for his generous and patient help with all the myriad things I'll probably never fully grasp. Thank You for making this book, and my website a reality! To my second-grade English teacher, **Trudi Egan**, I'm forever indebted, because it was YOU, all those years ago at Lake George Elementary School, who recognized that I was a writer. Thank You with all my heart, Mrs.

Egan. Thanks also to Team DDPYOGA member **Steven McEvoy** for your invaluable advice in how to self-publish. And to my wonderful nutritionist, **Nancy Guberti**, for helping take my already much-improved health to a higher level!

And a special note of Gratitude to **Chef Suvir Saran**, who taught me through example, the art of honoring myself and food…in that order. Your amazing cookbooks and approach to Life set my healing in motion that fateful day in 2008 when I visited you and Charlie at Masala Farm on assignment. Thank You, Suvir!

To the members of Team DDPYOGA, thank you for supporting me along my journey, especially in the beginning when I was feeling rather low, and needed it most. What a gift it is to have an instantaneous network of cheerleaders. Your presence and support continue to inspire me: to stay connected to the community, do better, and meet new challenges.

I also owe a debt of thanks to the Big Beautiful Women in the public spotlight whose confidence taught me to be proud of who I am - no matter what the scale said: **Roseanne Barr, Mo'Nique, Nancy Timpanaro-Hogan, Rosie O'Donnell, Conchata Ferrell, Totie Fields, and Oprah Wintrey** - the light you exuded when society said you shouldn't, helped me exude mine.

I want to thank my friends who were there for me during the thick and thin stages. You know who you are. You saw me for ME, and not my size, and that made an irrevocable difference in my life. And to all the 'friends,' former co-workers, classmates, school bullies, and strangers who looked down on me, took a cheap shot because you

5

could, and in some cases, deliberately humiliated me simply because you didn't like how I looked...I'm vetoing the predictable 'thanks for the adversity because it made me stronger' soliloquy. If I had to relive it all, I'd choose the happy childhood option. But since I'm still standing, I may as well send a pearl of great price your way by saying: *It's never too late to redeem your soul.*

And closer to home, I thank my family, immediate and extended, who were witness to all the 'dead years' I was shut down, trapped, and not really my true self. Thanks to my Mother, **Margaret McComas Morris** for surviving all the unpleasantness. My obesity and food addiction was surely an unexpected derailment for a mother. I'll bet it wasn't in the motherhood script you envisioned when you were decorating my nursery, and there was no manual for dealing with it once it unfolded. I'll probably never fully know how it hurt your heart as a mother to see me so unhappy, but now I can say, we survived it! And I Thank God you are enjoying this new chapter with me. Ditto for my siblings, **Dory, Mike,** and **Jeff,** who got their share of viewing the underbelly of human nature while I was, ahem, maturing. Thanks for hanging in, and for your forgiving natures. A big Muchas Gracias to **Antonio Ruiz** for giving me the necessity of unconditional acceptance when I needed it most desperately. To my Angelic cousin, **Anne Lundahl Higgins**, for your unwavering support of both my journey and my recipes - Your loving comments and pats on the back mean so much to me. And to the newest additions to my family: **Bill and Zach Duckman**...The Duckmen - I Love You - and not only because you're such willing test-drivers for the new recipes I invent! Chef Bill, my Jewish King, much of the inspiration in this cookbook comes from your passionate genius. I could not have written this cookbook without your input. You make

6

my life more delicious in so many ways. And to The Zachster, thanks for giving me a gift I never knew I was missing - until Jan. 13, 2012.

And to those who have passed before me: Thanks go to my **Aunt Alice Snively Winsor** for believing in my ability to be a writer; to my grandfather, **Donald Emory McComas** for being a prolific and sensitive writing role model; to my grandmother, **Edith Knabb McComas**, who taught me discipline and patience; to my beloved **Aunt Mary Frances Morris Garlick**, who walked the path of struggle with me, from you I learned what it means to live with gusto. And to my father, **Barr S. Morris**, who never got to see the newly minted, transformed version of his daughter: your life and what you taught me helped me get here. How I wish I could prepare you a meal made from this book. We would sit down to a bowl of Bill's New England Clam Chowder, then maybe a bit of cherry cobbler topped with coconut whipped cream for dessert. You'd marvel at how good everything tastes, and then probably do your own personal version of rejoicing when I told you how foods like this had a direct hand in my transformation.

What all the years of trial and error have taught me is there's no one answer to living in balance, but good, clean food is a big part of the mosaic. Loving food, preparing it with TLC, looking forward to an evening meal or post-workout snack keeps me sane, happy, and on track. I finally did it, Dad, I finally did it. I built a house of bricks. It's real this time. And I'm never going back.

Forward

I remember the first time I heard about Stacey Morris. Terri Lange had sent me an email letting me know that there was a woman on Team DDP YOGA who had lost 30 pounds during her first two months. Terri knows I love to call my team members to give them extra motivation when they demonstrate they're putting the work in. So I called...and I thought Stacey was going to crash her car when she realized it was me. Once I realized she was driving I asked her to pull over, and we talked for 20 minutes.

After hearing her story, I encouraged Stacey to go Gluten/Wheat/Dairy-Free. Stacey let me know straight out she was a Cheese Head and this was going to be a challenge because she pretty much lived on cheese. But when I told her she could still eat sheep or goat cheese, she was more willing to listen. From my years of experience in working with people with weight issues, I've realized that pretty much anyone who is 80 pounds or more overweight seems to have a problem with Gluten/Wheat/Dairy. For some reason their bodies don't know how to process these foods. And I personally eat this way to rid myself of as much inflammation as possible, not to mention I feel 15 years younger! The fact that eating Gluten/Wheat/Dairy-Free keeps me lean is just an added bonus.

With Terri's help we convinced her to give it a try, explaining the importance of making this new way of eating her lifestyle because diets never work! The harder Stacey worked, the more I wanted to help her, and the more results she saw. Terri and I loved getting monthly photo updates from Stacey of her shrinking size. And because Stacey loves to cook, we also were sent her amazing gluten- and dairy-free recipes, which we both love and continue to use.

I believe this book is for everyone! I know I'll use the recipes within, and will suggest this book to everyone I know because the recipes are definitely healthy; but most importantly, they taste Amazing! And it's just another example of Stacey putting the work in. She didn't want to settle for healthy; she needs what she eats to taste great! And with the help of Stacey's man Chef Bill, these recipes are also made with Love.

As I write the forward to Stacey's book, I'm reminded of how life is funny... Stacey came to Team DDPYOGA, like most people, looking for inspiration. Today she is one of the most inspiring people, not only on the site...Stacey is one of the most inspiring people I know, and that's saying something! What I admire most is she didn't just end the work once the weight was gone. Stacey continues to pay it forward with the inspirational blogs on her website and for *The Huffington Post*. She also co-hosts my show on DDP Radio every Wednesday evening, reaching out and helping people on all levels, and leading by example.

Stacey dropped over 180 pounds in 18 months, but more importantly, she has kept it off. How? Read on, and you'll see. Stacey keeps it off because she has become a gluten- and dairy-free home-taught chef. Stacey lives it... She walks the talk...and she Loves it!

As a mentor, I couldn't be any prouder.
       - Diamond Dallas Page
       Founder of DDPYOGA

In my many years of practicing nutritional and functional medicine, I have become a medical detective utilizing functional medicine lab testing to gain insight into one's health and uncover the root causes of one's illness and issues.

In the current state of increasing rates of obesity, diabetes, cardiovascular diseases, degenerative disorders, autoimmune, depression, everlasting fatigue, hormonal imbalances, adrenal overload in all ages, understanding the basics of healthy eating will provide profound and everlasting health benefits to anyone willing to try new foods and remove unhealthy eating habits.

The fact is we are definitely a product of what we eat. Breaking down our food into usable nutrients and absorbing them is crucial to our well-being. Incorporating an anti-inflammatory diet can assist the body in reducing inflammation, acid, and illness. The main culprits are wheat and dairy products because they cause inflammation, and if one cannot breakdown their peptides, havoc sets in.

Many individuals have problems breaking down the proteins that are in the dairy, called caseins; while the protein in wheat, barley, rye, and spelt flours are called gluten. Illness occurs when the incomplete breakdown of the gluten or casein passes the intestines as peptide chains and enters into the bloodstream, passing the blood-brain barrier. The incomplete breakdown turns into casomorphines from the casein and glutomorphines from the gluten, and transforms into an opiate. Opiates can cause the following side effects: clouded mental functioning, insomnia, diarrhea, impaired social connection, blocking of pain messages, dilated pupils, inflammation on the stomach lining, and depression.

It is a vicious cycle that never ends. Eating foods that cannot breakdown properly results in inflammation, leaky gut syndrome, skin disorders, depression, weight issues, food cravings, behavioral and mental issues.

Research has proven the importance of a GFCF diet (gluten-free and casein-free) for many of the following conditions: Autism Spectrum Disorders, Celiac, Depression, Weight-Loss, Psoriasis, Migraines, Multiple Sclerosis, Crohn's Disease, Schizophrenia, Ulcerative Colitis, Chronic Diarrhea Cystic Fibrosis.

Take heart, though, because there is hope.

Through this book, Stacey Morris has brilliantly offered you the means to make you aware of healthy, yummy foods that will nourish your body, and mind. From her insight and amazing recipes, you will be able to transcend your current eating regime into a healthier one while not compromising taste or enjoyment, as you assist your body in healing.

Educate and empower yourself. Let Food Be Thy Medicine and not Thy Poison.

- Nancy Guberti, nancyguberti.com
Biomedical Nutritionist, Functional Medicine Specialist, MS, CN

What Others Are Saying About Clean Comfort:

"Stacey Morris writes in an incredibly powerful way. Her honesty, transparency and vulnerability are inspiring to those trying to make changes in their lives. Her recipes are wonderful, comforting, and good for you. This book will nourish your body and spirit and provide sound knowledge for the mind. It will help you own your life!"
 - SRMcEvoy - www.bookreviewsandmore.ca

"I discovered Stacey Morris on the DDPYOGA website, and immediately became a follower of her "Hungry for the Truth," blog on Facebook. In Stacey, I found a mentor who I could identify with on many levels. Not only is she incredibly knowledgeable about sustaining lasting weight loss and healthy nutrition and cooking, she also lives her life in an authentic, conscious manner. Stacey is so open and honest about her own personal transformation experience, that after having read her story, I realized that I too, could do the same thing. Anyone who seeks to make changes in their life would benefit from Stacey's amazing journey."
 - Catherine Arnett, Statford, Conn.

I'm a big fan of Stacey's recipes because they're written from the perspective of someone who loves to indulge but also understands that every day can't be a big indulgence. Her recipes offer simple ways to create healthy and delicious food by incorporating the natural essences of ingredients and spices. Her recipe for red hummus inspired me to revisit and modify my own techniques for making hummus.
 - Jerry P. Papandrea, Albany, N.Y.

"I've used more than several of these recipes and ideas. Stacey

is inspiring and motivational in her weight loss success. From dealing with my own weight loss journey, she taught me that you can achieve your weight loss goals without sacrificing the taste and pure joy of eating delicious food."
- Michael Mullins, Dover, N.H.

"Stacey Morris combines wisdom and a dedication to healthy eating into some of the most delicious recipes I've ever tasted. Her cookbook is a must-have for anyone who wants to eat healthfully, but wants their food to taste as if they weren't!"
- Liz Collins, Chicago, Ill.

"I have been following Stacey and her recipes since I got on the DDPYOGA program. I asked my mom to make the Power Pesto and the whole family loves it. We're both very thankful to have come across her recipes and would definitely love to try out more."

- Johan Yusof and Farah Sulaiman, Kuala Lumpur, Malaysia

"Stacey's recipes show that you can eat foods that are healthy, tasty, and satisfying!"
- Gloria R., Glens Falls, N.Y.

Clean Comfort Part I:
The Foundation Before The Food
or
Inner Healing Always Precedes
Outer Healing
By Stacey Morris

Contents:

Food: How It Began For Me

This book is created for people like me in mind. If you're like me, you're an exceptional lover of food. You have, on more than one occasion in your lifetime, loved food a little too intensely. This may have resulted in excessive time, thought-energy, and cash being channeled in the direction of the enjoyment of food. If you're like me, this has resulted in the unfortunate circumstance of excess weight. I use the word unfortunate not because there's anything morally wrong with bearing excess weight. For me, it simply wasn't fun. Extra poundage was an unfairly high tax Mother Nature levied against me for doing something so simple and enjoyable. Was it that wrong?

Well, I suppose, on some level it must have been. Things must have gone decidedly awry for me and food when I went from a chubby kid to a fat teenager to an obese adult. This did not happen in one singularly straight path. There were countless and agonizingly difficult go-rounds with dieting, starting with my first at age 8, when I raced to the table one Saturday afternoon only to discover my place-setting had not a steaming bowl of Spaghetti-O's, but cold tomato slices and a scoop of cottage cheese.

I intensely disliked my fat and the embarrassment it caused me: at school, family reunions, and in the dressing room at Sears in 5th grade, where I could be found turning an uncomfortable shade of crimson beneath my mother's disapproving gaze as I tugged women's-department slacks over my stomach. But even more than that, I disliked dieting, the separation from food and pleasure that I began enduring on a semi-regular basis for the next 35 years. Sometimes I took the task on willingly, believing that this time my self-loathing and disgust had accrued to an avalanche powerful enough to topple, once and for all, my unending desire for food, for its texture, taste, and hypnotically soothing powers.

Food was an immediate response to life's more perplexing questions for which I had no answer: Why was I shy? Why was the bully-boy on the school bus obsessed with humiliating me? Why was it so hard to talk to classmates without my

15

cheeks turning red? Why did I feel so much shame over who I was? Why did I count the minutes until recess was over while other kids laughed on the swing sets and dangled from the monkey bars?

Another part of the problem with food and me was it was assigned a moral value early on in my life and largely forbidden. Treats such as cookies and potato chips were squirreled away out of my reach, or sometimes sequestered to an undisclosed location in the house and disguised as sewing kits or Christmas decoration storage boxes to keep me from prying into them and gratifying a hunger that was both physical and emotional in origin. I was a maturing child with a naturally active appetite to keep up with the growth spurts. But I was also chubby and this alarmed the adults around me. My guess is that the chubbiness was nothing more than a baby fat phase that would have evened itself out by my teens, but it's all hindsight now. My well-meaning parents thought the best course of action was to nip it in the bud, so my food intake was controlled and obsessed over. Even the babysitters were given the mandate. We all know how well prohibition does not work. Any fruit declared forbidden sets up the chase for it, the thrill of the acquisition, the ever-obsessive hunt to claim what is being withheld. My parents, years later, confided they blamed themselves for my weight. On more than one occasion they wondered if it was something they had done to bring on the imbalance. They sensed a looming problem and handled it in a way that seemed logical. It was the '70s. There were no support systems, handbooks, or talk shows that delved into the human psyche as there are today. I could blame so many people for the ever-strengthening love-hate vortex that grew around food. Most often, I started with myself and silent rounds of recrimination for not standing up to bully-boy, or the mean girls at school.

Four decades later, I have not the desire or energy to untangle all the cords that got me to where I eventually ended up: on a doctor's scale January 5, 2009, staring at the digital proclamation of 345 pounds. The bumpy ride of my childhood was only a precursor to my tumultuous relationship with food. It was a cyclonic journey that had me binge-eating alone in my

16

car on a regular basis. Eating at home was never a comfortable endeavor, so my car became a silent womb of safety and relief. I can still smell the French fry steam from the open paper bag of fast food. Always, that greasy mist was the enticing precursor to ingesting the bag's contents: the largest size of everything I loved on the menu. I'd inhale the burger-fry steam as if it were a life-saving vaporizer because it reassured me that relief was only seconds away. And the steam also irrevocably seeped into my car's upholstery, the way nicotine clouds permanently etch their presence into the fibers of a smoker's car. The interior of my beat-up, third-hand Oldsmobile always bore the faint aroma of my crutch. Fast food was my salvation. It tasted good when nothing else in my life did. I could get a bag of the goods without ever leaving the driver's seat of my car. And eat it in peaceful privacy, with no one watching or judging me. Sometimes I'd turn the radio up to drown out the sound I didn't care to listen to: my jaws grinding away mechanically, and not just grinding the cheeseburger. The grinding was a distraction from the rage, and the sorrow and the loneliness I pushed back into the dark underground cavern of unacknowledged feelings.

As always, there was the headless horseman arrival of the moment that interrupted the bliss: eating past the point of contentment. Relief vanished and in its place came disappointment. Each precious bite I tore from the cheeseburger meant another dent in my supply of salvation. And I'd ignore the large sigh my diaphragm emitted, signaling my stomach was full. My stomach may have had enough, but there was never enough happiness to go around for me...at least not from food, whether it was a box of donuts, a bag of cheeseburgers, or a towering sundae, dripping in chocolate syrup that left me stained and slurring in a sugar stupor. Those carefully planned moments with me, my car, and a fast-food bag defined happiness for me. And when the food was gone, so was the high, and I'd come crashing back to reality with a clumsy thud as I'd crumple the paper bag, wipe the grease off my hands, and dust away the confetti of sesame seeds, bun crumbs, and salt that covered my abdomen like a gravelly road.

And of course, the flip side of being out of control was eventually countered by ridiculous, insanely rigid regimens

17

of...I guess you could call it eating. Controlled eating, or diets, as they're commonly known are the magic elixir every overeater has grabbed tightly with both hands, applying the passionate cobra-squeeze of hope during the first 24 hours... if I lasted that long, which I often didn't. Wonder why? Maybe because it was an unrealistic way for someone like me to eat to begin with, and prescribed by an entity who didn't know me personally but purported to know what was best for anyone and everyone with a weight problem. No major shock that each and every diet left me crazed, bitter, and careening back to the drive-thrus. Is it any wonder that diets failed me? But oh, how I tried. The majority of the time, however, I ate ferociously, which resulted in steady, unfailing weight gain. By the time I was a senior in high school, my weight topped out at 230. During my post-high-school years, attempts to turn the tide included diets of every variety, health club memberships, aborted contracts with personal trainers, Overeaters Anonymous meetings, years of therapy, and a month-long check-in at a Los Angeles rehab for food addicts.

All it ever led to was more weight gain, compounded despair, and psychological exhaustion.

A Path To Follow

Why do I tell you all this? For starters, this is (as you've already guessed) more than a cookbook. In terms of ingredients included and ingredients avoided, these recipes follow a pattern that will provide you with a general road map, foodwise of how I found and maintained balance. Because of this, the recipe collection herein can't help but have a colorful story attached to it. People see my 'before' photos and want to know how I got that way. The same questions are asked of my 'after' shots. I've given you a brief synopsis of how I arrived at both. For those wanting to achieve a similar state to my 'before' shots, it's quite simple: eat copious amounts of foods laden with gluten, sugar, and cow-dairy (preferably till you feel so trash-bag-stuffed, you have to go recline on a Lazy-Boy), and repeat as needed.

If you're where I was in 2009 and want to get weight off, I'm not going to toy with you and suggest it's as simple as preparing my recipes. My recovery from binge eating and lifelong obesity was a mosaic of solutions. As an emotional eater, it was imperative that I face my demons and get to the root of what was sending me running from reality. That, my food-loving friends, takes time. Also required was a commitment to eject myself from the couch and get moving. Thanks to DDPYOGA, I didn't have to go very far from my lounging place of choice. Through regular application of the DVD workouts, I got physically fit in the comfort and privacy of my living room.

Ah, but the food...that was the Achilles heel that had plagued me from the start. The tempting, off-limits, and hedonistic substance that always won, and ruined every ounce of progress in the end. OK, hold up! Who wrote that script, and who says it has to be that way? I knew if I were to make changes I would want to live with, I must summon the courage and mental agility to question the status quo. Was food my enemy? Did it really hold Svengali-like control over my mind? Not really. It was I who'd chosen to misuse it. And it was I who could repair the relationship. But first, I had to fire a few experts. And I can't even honestly call them well-meaning experts because the only interest they ever had in me was their financial gain. So...diet industry - you're fired! You've been nothing but a thorn in my side, and because of the unrealistic way of life you

19

prescribe, have actually damaged my relationship with food and made me fatter. Food industry, get outta my face. And take your manipulative jingles and gaggle of character-actors who portray happy families with you. Most of what you're peddling have been outright lies, or amoral exaggerations at best. That 'balanced breakfast' you refer to in cereal ads? Tried it for years. All it did was make me hungry 25 minutes later. And news flash, we humans really don't get exponentially more graceful and strong by drinking milk intended for a four-legged bovine.

The crucial point I'm making is, certain foods pushed on me by big business hurt, rather than helped me. I have photographic evidence of me looking like a Sumo wrestler to prove it. Certainly, I had a hand in getting myself to 345 pounds, but in all my attempts to change my body and get rid of fat and feel more in balance, the only time I ever saw lasting change was when I cut gluten and cow dairy from my diet. That's how I eat now, and I'll never go back. Giving up gluten was really quite easy for me because there's a treasure trove of alternatives on the market, as well as foods such as rice, potatoes, and quinoa, which have always been gluten-free.

Cheese was a little more of a challenge, primarily because I love it so much. But when I cut the cord, I was astounded at how much more energy I had, and how rapidly the weight began to peel off. Still, every now and then, I dip back in... literally, at say, an Italian restaurant known for their Alfredo sauce. Within the hour, my stomach and digestive track rebel, and there are usually cramps involved. And this from a woman who literally *lived* on cream cheese. There are some (including my nutritionist, Nancy Guberti) who believe it's best to cut cheese out entirely because of casein, a protein that is often aggravating and difficult to digest. I've found that goat and sheep cheese don't sideline me the way cow dairy does, so I eat them in moderation. There's no doubt that cheese is delicious, but if you look at most cultures outside of the United States, they relegate cheese more as a condiment than a primary protein source. That makes a great deal of sense to me, so that's my approach to enjoying dairy: It's a treat, not a regularly visited food group.

As with countless other people on a gluten and dairy-free path I have spoken with, you will very likely look and feel better after giving these two ingredients the pink slip. How a person eats is as individual as their fingerprint and this book isn't about telling you how to eat. Can't stand fish? Then don't force yourself then. Not a sit down breakfast eater in the morning? That's cool. But I would advise packing a protein and healthy fat-laden snack for mid morning. It helps tremendously to have peanut butter and crackers, avocado slices, or a handful of walnuts and dried cranberries for when hunger comes calling. Eating foods you enjoy, even love, is essential to staying on a healthy path. But I had to get very clear with myself in terms what exactly it was I wanted. What mattered most to me... getting out of the 300s once and for all, or the taste of cream cheese? Fitting into an airplane seat again or stuffing myself with Italian bread and butter till I was groggy with carb overload? You get where I'm going with this point. I could not realistically expect change physically while keeping my repertoire of quantities, flavors, and textures intact. This may seem an obvious point but it's often the first protestation made when the words 'gluten free' come out of my mouth.

Here's a better way to look at it. Don't view it as *giving up* gluten and cow dairy, but rather, *trading up*. I traded up from wheat-based breads and crackers to breads, crackers, and cookies made without gluten. I traded up from processed cow cheese and milk to artisanal Manchegos and Chevres and sumptuous glasses of almond and sunflower seed milk. And you have not LIVED till you've tried whipped cream and rice pudding made from coconut milk.

What This Book Is Not

This book is not meant to resemble a diet in any way, but rather an outline of how I went from chronic binge-eater to someone who now eats according to hunger cues, physical activity (or inactivity as the case may be), and yes...PASSION. I knew early on when I began making changes and tailoring a way of eating that suited my palate and my health that I had to honor my passion for food. It was a part of me and it wasn't going anywhere.

Much like someone transgendered who feels born in the wrong body, I tried to no avail to MAKE myself become someone who was dispassionate about food. But it didn't feel natural... it simply wasn't who I was. I tried reforming the passionate pleasure-seeker through dieting and becoming very basic and strict with food choices. At my most extreme, I reasoned it was far more practical to simply yank food from the equation altogether and make attempts at subsisting on packets of powder that I'd blend into pasty, insipid versions of chicken noodle soup or scrambled eggs. I don't recall ever feeling as lifeless or depressed as I did during the 13 days I lived this way. I was so frustrated and crazed, I felt I might be dangerously close to committing a homicide. So, in the interest of staying out of prison, I threw the remaining powder packets away, defeated and about $300 poorer, I might add.

Because this is not a book about dieting or manipulating you or food in any way, there will be no lists of rules involving things such as:

Thou shalt not eat (even a morsel of) food after 7 p.m.
Thou shalt remember that fruit is forbidden after 3 p.m.
Thou shalt weigh thyself once a week (more often if thou prefereth a greater multitude of neurotic voices in thy head)
Thou shalt count and record thy fat grams
Thou shalt eat foods you truly enjoy but once per week, and it shall be called the CHEAT DAY because thou art transgressing.
Thou shalt eat no more than 1,500 calories per day and count each calorie as thou ingesteth it.
Thou shalt remember that being unhappy with one's appearance is a vow to be kept sacred.

I'm being a little dramatic with the list of commandments, but there can be no doubt that diets are oppressive. Anyone besides me know the intimate agony of "the last meal"? You know, the last good-tasting meal you get to enjoy before embarking on another voyage to the epicenter of deprivation? I decided that this time around, no "last meal" would be necessary, because I intended to enjoy this voyage. It would be a journey that struck a balance between gluttony and austerity. I wouldn't be climbing the walls waiting for the agony to end. Instead, I'd be in a comfortable groove of learning to live with both less and more:

* Less trance eating and more awareness
* Less pre-fab and fast food and more whole foods I cook myself
* Less stuffing myself and more listening to when I'm satisfied
* More nutrient-rich foods and beverages and fewer empty calories
* More food from the produce aisle and less food from the canned aisle
* More time devoted to food-prep and less money invested in convenience foods
* More physical activity and less couch-dwelling
* More greens and less whites (as in dairy and simple carbs)

Herewith is a brief outline for a typical day of eating and moving for me. I share it because I get regular queries through my website wondering how I got the weight off, what I eat, what percentage of my food intake is organic and GMO free, how much I exercise, etc.

Cabbage broth, sautéed greens, and carrots aren't my first choice. They just aren't. But I eat them even though I don't love them because it's a pact I've made with myself to put healthy things in my body. And because I eat plenty of healthy foods that I actually LOVE such as avocados, eggs, macadamia nuts, almonds, rice pudding, pan-seared salmon, tomato bisque, black bean chili...I'm sated enough and realize the scales of justice are balanced.

23

I'm not 100% anything: Vegan, gluten free, dairy free, or sugar free. For the vast majority of the time I eat gluten-sugar- and dairy-free. As for the vegan side of the equation, I often eat that way. Sometimes, I'm actually seized with vegan urges. And I roll with the carnivorous urges as well...I guess if I didn't love meatballs so much, I might become a vegan. I love vegan recipes and the way I feel after eating a vegan meal, but doing it 100% of the time is just not for me. I enjoy fish, eggs, Chevre, Manchego, and yes, the occasional serving of meatballs with marinara sauce far too much to give them up.

A Day in the Life

Overall, I'm more mindful of everything, not just food intake and exercise. I'm more dialed into my body in general vs. my eating days when I was deliberately disconnected. During a binge, it was as if the food wasn't going into my body, but to some convenient warehouse in a different time zone. As an emotional eater, I still have a tendency to want to comfort myself with food when the going gets tough, so I do have to make a concerted effort to be aware of feelings and FEEL them.

Nowadays, I begin my day with some quiet time in the a.m. and some light stretching. Later on, I make time for a DDPYOGA workout. My favorites are Below The Belt, Mix Tape, and Strength Builder because they pack a lot of moves in a compact amount of time (28-38 minutes). The fact is, in order to maintain my weight, I have to make time to work out. There's no magic bullet to keeping it off, no finish line to cross. Garden-variety maintenance is what it takes. As I write this, I'm in my 50th year. I look and feel better at age 50 than I did at age 25. There is no price that can be put on that kind of wealth. Investing in my well-being with time, energy, and cash has paid off beyond my wildest dreams. When I was 300 pounds plus for two decades, I'd daydream about how fantastic it would be to be a size 16-18 again. That's all I wanted. And it was so out of reach for so long. Now I'm a size 6-8, and I'm not playing the 'look at me!' numbers game...but it's a fascinating study in what can happen when you let go of outcomes, take care of yourself, and see what happens.

If I'm having a stressful day, or need to take a breather and get away from the computer, I won't do a full workout, but some of the more restorative moves like Broken Table, Diamond Cutter (wonderful for the spine), Hood Ornament and other one-legged poses which are great for balance and core strength.

As for food, I take my cues mostly from hunger. There's no weighing, measuring, or calorie-counting, but I pay attention to portion size, especially where things like rice, cereal, and pasta are concerned, because I can eat larger amounts of those and not even feel it.

The Truth About Eating Well:

Eating well is a Physical, Psychological, and Spiritual Endeavor.

Part of letting go of my indiscriminate binge-eating involved two things: 1) getting myself on solid psychological ground so I could face my demons and get to the root (actually it was a tangled clump of roots) of what was driving me to overeat; and 2) playing the 'weighing the options' with food by asking myself: 'Does It Matter?'

Naturally, the diet industry and women's magazines won't tell you that tackling No. 1 is a years' long process. Not the news you want to hear, I know. But wouldn't you rather get some truth, rather than sugar coated lies and half-truths from someone with a financial agenda? How you handle No. 1, if you need to handle it at all, will be up to you. Listen to your gut on this one. If you feel it's time to do some digging in the dirt and you're ready, go in. Get support. Be kind to yourself along the way. Confronting the past and long-dormant feelings can be a very intense ride at times, but you will come out feeling freer and much more empowered.

While No. 1 is an inner journey, No. 2 is all about the external process of eating. Not just eating, but upgrading, fine-tuning, and cleaning up food choices. And about that all-important question, 'Does It Matter?' Here's what I mean: I realized I liked diet soda OK but wasn't really crazy about it. Does it matter if I cut back on it, or cut it out completely? The answer was no, and I switched to seltzer with lemon. Eventually I fine-tuned it further and made hot tea my secret hydrating and cleansing weapon.

I liked pizza, but I didn't *love* it...not the way I do fried oysters. Besides, pizza is such a trap for foods that are highly caloric and not great for me, like cheese and processed meats. Does it matter to me if I rarely eat pizza? Nope, but fried oysters DO matter! I'm wise enough to know I can't live on 'em though. They're a treat. And that was a big part of my growth: silencing the toddler who had been on an extended (20-year) temper tantrum, insisting she would eat as much of what she loved, whenever she damn well felt like it. Seemed great in theory. But after a few years of this, I could no longer fit in theater seats. I was so far gone into a pattern of self-destruction that I ceased caring. I put myself on the mailing list of every plus-sized clothing catalog I could find, made sure I had an arsenal of black-stretch leggings at my disposal, and washed my hands of any resolve to change.

Thank God Life finally intervened. No more temper tantrums. And no more unreasonable deprivation either. Now I walk the middle road. I eat well: fresh or frozen fruit in the morning, real food throughout the day, supplements prescribed by my nutritionist, quality herbal tea, and treats when I really want them so I'm psychologically satisfied. And I eat when I'm physically hungry. That's the infallible guide we're all born with, and all too often we're taught to ignore or second-guess it. I don't adore vegetables, but eat them because I want better health and a balanced body. Some vegetables, like cauliflower hash, I actually enjoy. And on days when I need to up the raw quotient, I stuff some raw spinach down my gullet as if it were medicine - it's over quickly, I've given my body something it needs, and have not played any mentally taxing games with myself that this is something I should be liking - I just *do* it.

Eating techniques I use to keep the weight off
1. Avoiding gluten and cow dairy
2. Limiting simple carbs (rice, pasta, cereal) to one serving a day. I'm not super rigid with this. There are, of course days when I have more, but the majority of the time, it's once a day.
3. Eating for pleasure. How could I do this long-term if I didn't have good-tasting meals to look forward to?
4. Avoiding or limited processed foods, especially hot dogs, salami, etc., as they tend to contain chemicals, sodium, and fluid-retaining nitrates.

How I handle cravings

First, I determine whether it's an emotional craving or a physical one. I know myself well enough to know when I'm reaching for food to avoid a feeling or distract myself from tedium. If that's the case, I take some time to deal with what's going on in the moment.

If it's a physical or biological craving, I'll go for it, but in moderation. I don't have a big sweet tooth - salty foods are my thing. I once lived on potato chips and clam dip. Not a very healthy combination. I get occasional cravings for it, but have devised an alternative that will satisfy my urge to eat something crunchy and salty while not wrecking my health and balance. Here's what I do instead: potato chips are gluten free and technically 'legal,' but remind me too much of binge eating, so I substitute Asian rice crackers. They're crisp, fat free, and get the job done. Traditional cream cheese is out of the question. I simply won't do that to my body anymore, so I use vegan cream cheese as the base for the clam dip. This is by no means considered health food, it's actually more of a psychological release, but I realized after all the dieting prisons I put myself in, there are valid and sacred times where it's necessary to eat simply for the pure enjoyment of it.

A Typical Day of Eating Goes Something Like:

Morning:
Hot tea and fruit in the morning on an empty stomach because it's very cleansing.

20 or 30 minutes later, eggs with sautéed vegetables such as spinach with garlic or cherry tomatoes. If I'm really in the mood for a treat, I'll have a gluten-free roll or bagel with it, but that's not the norm.

On days that I don't eat eggs in the morning, I'll have gluten-free hot cereal made with almond milk. I also add unsweetened shredded coconut, ground chia seeds, and some coconut oil. It's a cereal that's satisfying and very nutrient-dense.

Lunch:
Combinations include: Vegetable-based soup with rice or cubed potatoes as a starch; a crock of baked spicy lentils and rice; or a burger with no bun and a salad. And if I'm really feeling a legitimate craving: fried chicken (My all time favorite) with a side of cooked veggies or a salad.

Post-Work Out:
I choose whole, sometimes raw foods that pack a lot of nutrition but also taste good: nut butter on a rice cake; a small handful of almonds or walnuts, an avocado with rice crackers or gluten-free matzo, or a serving of 'chocolate mousse' made with avocado, stevia, and raw cacao powder - it's fabulous!

Dinner:
Very often it's salmon or sea bass with a side of vegetables. It could also be steak and vegetables, meatballs and vegetables, or if I'm not real hungry...a variety of vegetables: tomato and avocado salad, slices of baked eggplant or zucchini, a big bowl of homemade vegetable soup, etc. Lunch is usually bigger than dinner. And I seldom eat carbs at dinner.

'Dessert'

Because dinner's a modest meal, I tend to get hungry around 9 or 10 p.m. I have a pretty firm rule about not eating at night, my body's going into rest mode so it's really not required. However, being active and exercising means the hunger is usually legitimate. And evening is the one time of the day I crave sweets. My solution is an amazingly delicious protein drink that tastes like a chocolate milkshake. Ingredients are unsweetened vanilla almond milk, a scoop of vegan or egg white protein powder, a few dashes of super-foods such as Maca and Goji powder. It's a satisfying and nurturing way to close my day, not go to bed hungry, and do something kind to my body and soul.

Clean Comfort Part II:
Food...
Glorious (and clean!) Food

Breakfast
I'm giving breakfast its own category, a) because it's my favorite meal of the day, and b) like anything you do in the morning, it sets the tone for the remaining 23 hours. No other meal is as loaded with the pure potential of possibility as this one.

Fruit: First Things First
My fitness and nutrition mentors, Dallas Page and Terri Lange both urged me to eat fruit on its own in the morning. "I do it because it's a shower for my colon," sang Terri, in one of her typically sunny e-mails where she would answer my questions on food and nutrition at length. That was enough of a visual for me to get the picture: fruit on its own, without proteins, carbs, or fats to impede its passage, is a fantastic cleanser for the digestive track. Not to mention a great wake-up call for your body, sending a welcome wagon of vitamins, natural sugar, and other nutrients to the blood stream. Depending on the season, I'll start out with fresh fruit that's locally sourced like apples, cherries, pears, or berries. When the harvest is over I'll indulge in oranges, grapefruit, mango, papaya, or bags of frozen berries. And when the weather's really cold, I love nothing more than to bake a batch of fruit...it's fantastic. Whether my a.m. fruit is fresh, frozen, or baked, I usually wait 20-30 minutes before following up with cereal or eggs. Try it..I think you'll like it!

Baked Apples
Serves 2

Apple season where I'm from in upstate New York means every square inch of our kitchen and sometimes dining room, is laden with the bounty of Devoe's, our neighborhood orchard. In other words, there are far too many to eat in their raw, crunchy state. So what's a Recovering American to do? Pies have their place, but they're not really early-morning fare. Instead, my gorgeous turquoise tagine comes to the rescue. A tagine is a round baking dish with fitted, cone-shaped lid that is popular in North African and Middle Eastern cooking. It's conical conducts condensation and returns it to the bottom of the dish, imbuing its contents with a delicate gulf stream of steam. The result: falling-off-the-bone meat, velvety soft potatoes, and in this case, fragrant, juicy piles of sliced apples with an almost sauce-like texture. The beautiful part is it's achieved in about 30 minutes and without an ounce of effort expended on mashing and stirring. If you want the apple slices with a little more heft, cut the cooking time by about 10 minutes. The modest calorie count of these apples coupled with the cleansing, energizing results of fruit in the morning on an empty stomach could further distract you from the realm of pies. Truly.

The one caveat (in a rush-rush world) is the time investment: this dish isn't an instant one. And I know you weren't thinking about using a microwave...right? If you're pressed for time because of the morning commute (which I sometimes am, even though I work from home) simply bake them the night before. They're fine in a cooled off oven overnight. All they require the next morning is 5 or 10 minutes at 300 degrees. Baked apples are a one of the most delicious things to come out of our oven since gluten-free macaroni and cheese. And it's enticingly simple to make:

Ingredients:
4 large or medium-sized apples or 5 smaller ones
Optional: a few dashes of cinnamon, nutmeg, or pumpkin pie spice

Instructions:
Preheat oven to 340 degrees. Slice apples into disc-like slices, cutting around the core (if you live in a suburban setting, reserve cores for the squirrels – they LOVE 'em). The shape of the slices really doesn't matter because the fruit alchemizes into a chunky applesauce by the time it's done. Arrange slices in layers in the casserole dish. If desired, sprinkle layers with spices. Cover and bake for 30 minutes. Shut oven off and let apples sit in the oven another ten minutes. Remove and scoop into bowls. Enjoy!

Morning Glory: Baked Cherries

Serves 2

There was a time, circa the 80s through 2008 that breakfast for me comprised tow main ingredients: sugar and fat. These two key ingredients were augmented by either lots of white carbs or some heavy form of protein such as sausage, corned beef hash, or bacon. I loved things like a stack of heavily buttered toast with bacon and eggs, or a half a loaf of gooey cherry cheese strudel. Then I'd wash it down with either a glass of orange juice or a cup of coffee lightened liberally with that fake creamer. I look back now and wonder how I functioned the rest of the day. No wonder I was such a slug - I was eating food that completely threw my digestive system into prophylactic overdrive.

When the reformation of my eating habits and food choices began in 2009, it was all about finding the middle ground and focusing on what I CAN enjoy, while still keeping things like blood sugar, waistline, and energy level in balance. So, while I love the taste of fruit baked in a pie, cookie, or strudel, I didn't love what the extra calories, fat and carbs were doing for me. Why not keep the fruit in the picture and ditch the rest? And that's how baked cherries were born. I love baking in clay pots. It gives meats a falling-off-the-bone quality and works magic on stews, lentils, rice pudding, and leftover pasta. Clay pots also do the same for fruit, whether it's cherries, berries, or fragrant layers of sliced apples. I'm not convinced clay pots and tagines are alchemists. If you don't have one, it's no problem. A covered ceramic casserole dish will do nicely.

My Ayurvedic constitution is Kapha (see glossary), so maybe that's why I prefer warm foods vs. ice-cold. Baked fruit has the comforting quality of a dessert with none of the nutritional negatives. The heat, when applied gently and for the right amount of time, beautifully brings out the flavor, as well as a river of juices you just wouldn't get from fruit out of the fridge, or even at room temperature. Obviously, the most opportune time to bake fruit is when it's in season locally. But when apples, cherries, and berries aren't available at the farmers market, frozen fruit works quite well.

Ingredients & Instructions:
Preheat oven to 335. Place 3 cups of fresh cherries at room temperature in clay baking pot, tagine, or ceramic casserole dish. Bake for 30 minutes. Turn oven off and let sit in oven another 10-15 minutes. The result is pure Nirvana: The beauty and fragrance of a cherry pie minus the white stuff to wreak havoc with the blood sugar. The photos don't do their splendor justice, so you'll just have to try it out to see what I mean. Note: * If you're using frozen cherries or berries, change temperature to 300 and bake for 20 minutes, let sit in cooling oven for 10-15 minutes.

Blueberry Breakfast Parfait
Serves 1
As deep as my adoration of sunny side up eggs is, variety is the spice of life. This morning, my palate was calling for flavors and textures beyond that of sunny-side up eggs and caramelized onions. I usually eat carbs earlier in the day. It took some time and was a learning curve, but I I've generally transitioned away from the relatively empty-calorie cold cereals to the fibrous and nutritionally dense hot cereals.

I came up with this breakfast parfait one August morning when local blueberries were plentiful and a bowl of steaming hot cereal was unappealing. It had been months since I dipped into the bag of Bob's Red Mill Gluten-Free Steel Cut Oats in my cupboard...so I got busy. If soaked overnight, bullet-hard steel cut oats soften perfectly. Steel cut oats require pre-planning but they're so satisfying, it's worth the effort. This parfait is a fabulous breakfast loaded with flavor, complex carbs, fiber, and vitamins...plus a little calcium and protein. It's also perfect fuel before a workout. And may I say...Thank GOD for Bob's Red Mill. Their gluten-free products are reasonably priced and fantastic!

Ingredients:
2 cups fresh or frozen blueberries
1/4 cup Bob's Red Mill Gluten-Free Steel Cut Oats
1/4 cup Bob's Red Mill Flaked Unsweetened Coconut
1/2 cup goat's milk or coconut yogurt

Instructions:
Puree blueberries in a food processor until berries are liquidy but still a little chunky. Place in a saucepan and simmer on low heat uncovered for 30 minutes, stirring occasionally. The berries should be liquidy but with a little thickness. Turn off heat and add oatmeal and coconut, stirring thoroughly. Cover and let sit overnight. In the morning add yogurt and stir until blended. Serve immediately.

Optional:
Sweeten with a teaspoon of agave or a few drops of stevia.

Berry Bliss: A Better Way (to cleanse the colon)

Serves 2
Yes, I went there! But do note that I was tame in the phrasing. No need for gasp-worthy descriptions here, but let's face it, my recovery has been a blend of loving food and finding ways to have it work FOR me. Fruit in the morning on an empty stomach is inherently cleansing. So why not up the ante and enjoy a blast of berries? All berries are fantastic for you, but raspberries in particular are high in vitamins and low on the glycemic index, meaning they have a low sugar count. A bowl of fresh berries or glass of raspberries is a far better way for my money, to do a little house-cleaning. And since I'm of the belief that the river of digestion is meant to flow in one direction, I'm a major fan of the berry method. That plus

drinking a cup of a Senna Root-based tea every few months is all I need to keep things flowing in an orderly fashion.

Ingredients:
3 cups berries in any combination, either fresh or frozen (no sugar added)
1 tsp. coconut palm sugar or 6 drops stevia (berries can be tart)
1 tsp. lemon zest
1 Tbs. lemon juice
Purified water as needed
Optional: 3-4 ice cubes

Instructions:
Place all ingredients in a blender and blend for about a minute, or until smooth. Pour and enjoy.

Power to the Pudding (Power Pudding)
Serves 2
I can't get enough of Chia Seed Pudding and evolving variations thereof. The discovery of it stems from a sugar-cleanse I undertook under the guidance of Nancy Guberti, my nutritionist. Gone are the gluten-free cookie free-for-all's. In their place are treats with a far lower glycemic index. They're tasty, but they also do something for me. Case in point: this pudding recipe that I'm crazy about: its taste, texture, low calorie count, high nutrient count – everything! that I began tinkering with the recipe to include other healthy ingredients. Recent favorites include ground flax seed, ground chia seeds, shredded coconut, coconut flakes, various forms of protein powder, and hemp hearts (see glossary).
 There was a time when they were so new to the world, hemp hearts could only be bought online – now most health food stores carry them. The bag I found at Uncle Sam's is made by Manitoba Harvest.
This recipe requires no cooking, only overnight in the refrigerator to thicken. I eat a cup at a time, either in the morning or post-workout. If I'm wanting more sustenance, I add a scoop of egg white or hemp-based protein powder. And if I'm in the mood for more of a hot cereal, I add ground flax and

heat a cup on the stove.

Ingredients:

3 cups unsweetened almond milk (regular or vanilla)
6 tablespoons hemp hearts
6 tablespoons Chia seeds
1/2 cup unsweetened coconut flakes (I like Bob's Red Mill)
3 packets Stevia (or 2 tablespoons of agave)
1 tablespoon vanilla

Instructions:
In a large glass jar or tupperware container, blend all ingredients and mix thoroughly with a spoon or whisk. This is necessary to do for 2-3 minutes so the Chia seeds don't clump together. Refrigerate overnight. Serve chilled, at room temperature, or heated. For a variation, add a scoop of protein powder or 2 tablespoons ground flax seeds to a one-cup serving.

Hot Stuff In The Morning

If you're not a major fan of cream of rice or oatmeal, do what you must at the outset to make it taste delectable: sweeten it with molasses, honey, stevia, agave, brown sugar, whatever floats your boat. What's important is you're giving some healthy, whole grains a try, which is a far cry better for the body than the nearly fiberless cold cereals, or a bagel soaked in butter.

This next measure I take is optional, but I hope you'll try adding a few super foods to the mix. Hot cereal actually lends itself to absorbing a teaspoon or two of powdery super foods like maca, goji powder, ground flax or chia seeds, or a dollop of coconut oil. Chia and flax seeds are often marketed as whole seeds but I've heard from a number of sources (and it makes sense to me) that these poppy-sized seeds are so tiny, they can't be broken down in the digestive track like larger foods so they pass right through and so do the nutrients, unused. The solution is to grind them yourself in a nut or coffee grinder or buy them pre-ground.

Oh, and then there are the SPICES! The ones you'd flavor baking items with are truly an artist's palate where hot cereal is concerned: cinnamon, nutmeg, cardamom, turmeric, pumpkin pie spice, allspice. And they all have nutritional and antioxidant properties. YAY!

I can hear those on a tight schedule muttering about the time it must take to prepare. Sure it's more than a zap in the microwave, but cooked on medium-low (hot cereal burns easily so watch the flame and stir often) it's done in 10-15 minutes. My strategy for a little time-saving: Get all the ingredients together in a saucepan the night before. The grains soak and get nice and plump overnight in the milk (I use almond milk so spoilage isn't a factor) and cooking time's not as long.

So there you have it, one of my strategies for comforting yourself with carbs in a way that will enhance your body's functioning, not throw a monkey wrench into it.

Tropical Cornmeal Porridge
Serves 1

Ingredients:
Cornmeal
Almond Milk
1 dark, gooey-ripe banana
1 wire whisk

Instructions:
Follow instructions on the label for 1 serving, making sure to whisk often so it stays smooth. When the cornmeal and milk are thickened, add the banana and keep whisking. No need to precut. If it's super ripe it will dissolve without much effort.

Super Oatmeal with Goji Berries
Serves 1

Ingredients:
1 1/2 cups unsweetened almond, coconut, or sunflower seed milk
1/3 cup Bob's Red Mill Gluten-Free Oats
2 tablespoons ground flax or chia seeds
2 tablespoons hemp hearts
1/4 cup dried goji berries *
1/8 teaspoon salt
1/2 teaspoon vanilla
1 tablespoon coconut oil
Sweetener of choice: 1 tablespoon agave, honey, or coconut palm nectar. Or 8 drops of stevia.

* Dried goji berries are very tough (not soft like raisins) so this cereal recipe lends it self to an overnight soak. If you can, place all ingredients but sweetener in a small saucepan and soak overnight. In the morning, place covered over medium-low heat and cook for about 10-15 minutes or until desired thickness is reached. Stir occasionally. When done, mix in sweetener and serve immediately.

Gommy's 'Buttermilk' Pancakes

Serves 4-6

You may have guessed that this is inspired by my amazing (mother of 7, grandmother of 18 great-grandmother of 21, Edith McComas. We called her Gommy because that's how David, the first grandchild, eked out his pronunciation of Grandma as a tot. Every Christmas morning, the bustle and ebullient commotion of Gommy's pancake-making assemblyline made Grand Central Station look abandoned. Her buttermilk pancakes were both legendary and prize-winning. And they made it into the cookbook. Gommy's lightly aromatic stacks of buttermilk pancakes served with Jones sausage links (the only brand she'd consider using) were such a siren call, the guest list seemed to grow each year. In other words, a crowd of 30-40 wasn't unusual. My mom continued the tradition and my siblings and I grew up on Gommy's pancakes on Christmas morning. So you can imagine the conflict I felt that first Christmas of being gluten and dairy-free. Gommy's pancakes didn't just taste amazing - they were an emotionally embedded memory for mc. I decided there was no better time to (respectfully) play around with my grandmother's recipe, and the makeover below comes close. The key is to have the milk and eggs at room temperature, use real butter, and sift the dry ingredients together thoroughly.

Ingredients:
2 cups flour (1 cup chick pea flour, 1/2 cup white rice flour, 1/2 cup potato starch), double rising agents. extra egg
1 teaspoon baking powder
1 teaspoon baking soda
Scant tsp. salt
2 tablespoons agave or raw sugar
2 cups unsweetened almond milk + 2 tablespoons white vinegar *
OR 2 cups goat milk*
3 eggs *
3 tablespoons melted butter
1 teaspoon vanilla
* Left out overnight to get to room temperature

Instructions:
In a large mixing bowl, sift flour and other dry ingredients together thoroughly or whisk vigorously with a fork. In a separate bowl, thoroughly blend the milk, vinegar, and eggs, using a non-electric hand-mixer or fork (if you really want a workout). Add the wet ingredients to the large bowl and mix thoroughly with a whisk, scraping sides with spatula as necessary. Add melted butter and vanilla and mix some more. Coat a non-stick pan or cast iron skillet with light olive oil or cooking spray. Heat for 2 minutes on medium then cook pancakes 1 or 2 at a time (as pan space permits). Serve immediately, or hold on a foil covered platter in a warm oven.

Suggested toppings: spread a teaspoon or two of coconut oil (solid at room temperature) over each pancake and top with maple syrup. Or if you're watching sugar grams: coconut palm nectar, sugarless syrup, homemade cranberry sauce (see recipe), or all-fruit jam. For super decadence or a special occasion, add a dollop of coconut whipped cream! (see recipe in dessert section)

Coconut Pancakes
Serves 4-6

Ingredients:
2 cups flour (1 cup chick pea flour, 1/2 cup white rice flour, 1/2 cup potato starch)
1/4 cup ground, unsweetened coconut
2 teaspoons baking powder
2 teaspoons baking soda
Scant teaspoon salt
2 tablespoons Agave or coconut palm sugar
2 cups unsweetened almond milk, vanilla or regular*
3 eggs *
3 tablespoons melted butter
1 teaspoon vanilla
Coconut oil for frying
* Left out overnight to get to room temperature

Instructions:
In a large mixing bowl, sift flour and other dry ingredients together thoroughly or whisk vigorously with a fork. In a separate bowl, thoroughly blend the milk and eggs, using a non-electric hand-mixer or fork (if you really want a workout). Add the wet ingredients to the large bowl and mix thoroughly with a whisk, scraping sides with spatula as necessary. Add melted butter and vanilla and mix some more. Coat a non-stick pan or cast iron skillet with coconut oil. Heat for 2 minutes on medium then cook pancakes 1 or 2 at a time (as pan space permits). Serve immediately, or hold on a foil covered platter in a warm oven.

Suggested toppings: spread a teaspoon or two of coconut oil (solid at room temperature), followed by a drizzle of coconut palm nectar. If you're really feeling coconutty, add a dollop of coconut whipped cream!

Zucchini Quiche
Serves 4
Greens in the Morning? Yes! I'm always looking for ways to include more greens into my life in ways that don't feel like I'm grazing, herbivore-style, on mounds of cold leafy structures, which, even drizzled with the finest of extra virgin olive oils, still isn't enough of an enticement to cause me to enjoy salad. I just don't. If you do, God love 'ya – go at it! But me? My idea of getting greens down in a compatible way includes plenty of COOKING. Spinach sauteed with garlic, a hearty bowl of minestrone soup, or cauliflower puree are all examples of good times that can be had with fresh produce. And so is this next recipe, which I adapted from a reader recipe in my local newspaper. It's quick, has lots of greens, is a good source of protein, and has just the right ratio of simple carbs to make it a comfort food, in a totally non-destructive way.

Ingredients:
6 eggs
1/4 cup water
1 teaspoon onion salt
1/2 teaspoon pepper

2 large to medium zucchinis, shredded with a cheese grater
1 cup Gluten-Free All-Purpose Baking Mix (such as Bob's Red Mill, Namaste, Pamela's, or Bisquick…truth be told, I only had Bob's Red Mill GF Pancake Mix in the cupboard and it worked fine)
1 cup shredded Manchego (a hard sheep's milk cheese)

Instructions:
Preheat oven to 325. In a large mixing bowl, whisk eggs and water until fluffy and well-blended. Add salt and pepper and mix well. Fold in shredded zucchini until thoroughly mixed. Add the baking mix, 1/2 cup at a time until well blended with other ingredients. Add the shredded Manchego and mix thoroughly. Spray an 8×8 baking pan with cooking spray and pour egg mixture into it, spreading it evenly with a rubber spatula. Bake for 25 minutes, then check. If quiche still feels undercooked in the middle leave it in another five minutes before checking again. If it feels soft, but nearly done, oven can be shut off and it can sit in cooling oven for another ten minutes.

Poached Eggs with Asparagus
Serves 2
Poached eggs are one of my favorite things in the world. As much as I adore Eggs Benedict, this recipe is easier and lighter. It's a little detailed, so wait for a leisurely weekend morning to try it out. If you don't have the time or the patience for poaching, this recipe works just fine with fried eggs.

Ingredients:
Four eggs, cracked into separate small dishes (see method)
1 tablespoon apple cider vinegar
1/2 cup balsamic vinegar
1 teaspoon capers
10 asparagus stalks, grilled or blanched to al dente
1/4 cup peccorino cheese, shaved with a potato peeler
Salt and pepper to taste
Optional: dash of smoked paprika

Instructions:

Warm two oven-safe plates or ramekins in a 200-degree oven Cook Balsamic vinegar and capers sauce pan uncovered until reduced by half. Cover, turn off heat and keep warm. Prepare asparagus and lay stalks 1/4-inch apart on warmed plates. Return plates to oven while preparing eggs (see method below). When eggs are ready, set two poached eggs next to each other on top of asparagus. Drizzle equal amounts of balsamic mixture over eggs. Top with equal amounts of peccorino shavings and a small sprinkle of smoked paprika.

Poaching method: in either a shallow saucepan or high-sided skillet, bring 3-4 inches of water to a boil. Add vinegar. With a slotted spoon, create a swirling motion of the water. Immediately drop eggs in to swirling water, one at a time. Do not stir. Poach until whites have just turned white, not glassine. With a slotted spoon or mesh strainer, remove poached eggs from water and drain well.

Protein in Liquid Form: Be Not Afraid!

Among my dieting war stories, liquid protein fasts and meal replacements definitely rank in my Top 5 as the most harrowing. Propelled by nothing but willpower and self-hatred, I'd drift through the days (or in some cases hours) that I was able to confine myself to the calorically bereft way of existing. My only salvation: a watery glass of something that tried to resemble a chocolate malt. This was decades ago. Fortunately, the world of liquid protein has come a looong way, baby! And so have I.

I found myself in a state of amazement one afternoon after noticing I had actually chosen to have a protein drink for lunch rather than fix a meal. That I was in a hurry and heading out the door was part of the reason, but the other: I actually enjoy the taste, texture, and effect of the protein drinks I make. And by effect, I mean how it nourishes me, metabolizes in my system, and how it leaves me feeling, both physically and psychologically. The quality of ingredients have improved dramatically in recent years. This means there are protein drinks that taste good and DO good things for you. My favorite protein powders are hemp, pea protein and egg whites. Throw superfood powders, chia seeds, coconut oil, and raw cacao into the mix and you have a veritable celebration! You're doing something fantastic for your health and it won't leave you feeling abandoned and ripped off.

I replace meals this way only occasionally. Most of the time it's a post-workout snack or a dessert after dinner. And because I've worked on myself psychologically, I feel at peace and balanced enough to eat less and be OK with it, vs. wanting to strangle someone. It is in learning to genuinely love liquid forms of protein that I realized the truism that comfort and decadence are not one and the same. These drinks are truly comforting...and some are so delish, they could be categorized as decadent!

Another thing I learned: Not all chocolate is the same. Your body knows the difference between a drink made with raw cacao powder and an amalgamation of cocoa butter and refined sugar. In order to maintain my 180-lb. weight loss, I've had

48

to both make peace with food and give the pink slip to food choices which were not doing my body, mind, or spirit any favors.

I'm a firm believer that when you really want a piece of chocolate cake, there's simply no substitute. But let's get real, I can't be doing chocolate cake everyday, and it's not exactly nutritional anyway. But I do usually want the taste of chocolate in some capacity on a daily basis, and I want good nutrition, plus the privilege of remaining comfortably in my size 8 jeans. Remember (if you're old enough) when size 8 was THE standard? Now it's practically considered a plus size but lemme tell you, and no pun intended, I put no weight into that insane kind of thinking. So I'll pass on regular rounds of cookies, candy bars, cupcakes and other nutritional vagaries. A chocolate protein shake is by no means the same experience as a mountainous slice of double-layer cake, but it does the job. And by that I mean it satisfies physical hunger in a big way, delights my chocolate-craving taste buds, and keeps my progress intact.

Disappointingly, bottled protein drinks are the latest thing to be appropriated by the big food companies. You can find them everywhere now, from supermarkets to convenience stores. Only take the bottled option if you're in dire need. A far better choice is to concoct your own at home because it's more cost effective and you can control the quality.
Becoming a regular with protein drinks is a process. It may not be love at first gulp, but when you consider the benefits (and when you feel the supreme satisfaction of actually being nourished by something sweet and delicious, you just may end up like me and so many others, giving the prepackaged goodies a rest.

  * My protein powders of choice are Plant Fusion, Keto-Slim, and Jay Robb's Egg White, all in vanilla. I find vanilla to be the perfect blank canvas for incorporating other flavors such as berries, cinnamon, and the eternally worshipped chocolate...

Stacey's Liquid Chocolate Satisfaction
Serves 1

Ingredients:
8 ounces unsweetened vanilla almond milk
1 scoop vanilla protein powder
1 tablespoon raw cacao powder
1 teaspoon maca (a favorite superfood)
And if I'm feeling really racy, 1 tablespoon coconut oil
(optional)

Instructions:
Place all ingredients in a blender and blend for about 20
seconds or until smooth. Serve and feel nourished.

Chocolate Building Block Brew
Serves 1
This is perfect for an evening dessert. I prepare it most often on
dark winter nights, when I'm wanting an extra dose of comfort.
It's a good cup of hot chocolate, with the benefits of the muscle-
enhancing building blocks from a healthy dose of protein.

Ingredients:
1 1/2 cups unsweetened almond or coconut milk
1 tablespoon raw cacao powder
1 teaspoon vanilla
1 scoop vanilla protein powder

Instructions:
Place milk in small saucepan on medium-low heat. Cook
for five minutes, whisking occasionally. When milk is above
lukewarm, add remaining ingredients and whisk vigorously
until smoothly blended. Heat for another two minutes and serve
immediately.

Peanut Butter Pleasure
Serves 1

Ingredients:
1 1/2 cups unsweetened almond, sunflower seed or coconut milk
1 scoop protein powder
1-2 tablespoons peanut butter, or your favorite (cashew, almond, sunflower seed)
1 tablespoon maca
Optional: 3-4 ice cubes

Instructions:
Place all ingredients in a blender and blend for about 20 seconds or until smooth. Serve and feel nourished.

Maqui Madness
Serves 1
Maqui powder is a deep purple, nutrient-packed superfood high in antioxidants, Vitamin C, iron, anti-inflammatory compounds, and potassium. The name of this drink comes from the fact that I'm mad for Maqui's fruity flavor, which is unlike anything I've tasted, but reminds me of a cross between grape and cherry. Yes Virginia, there are days when I crave a fruity shake instead of chocolate, and this fits the bill deliciously.

Ingredients:
1 cup unsweetened almond milk
1 scoop protein powder
2 ounces espresso or strong coffee or 1 Tbs. granulated espresso powder
1 tablespoon maca

Optional: 3-4 ice cubes

Instructions:
Place all ingredients in a blender and blend for about 20 seconds or until smooth. Serve and feel nourished.

Tricks are for Goji Berries
Serves 1
Another superfood, the dried berries themselves are tart. The powder's flavor, however, as a gentle sweetness with a top note of Trix. Yes I said Trix. Though that sugar and dye-laden cereal is relegated to my eating past, I can't say I didn't adore the sweet, fruity taste of the stuff. This protein drink allows me to take my taste buds down memory lane while staying clean and on track. Bonus: goji powder is high in amino acids, anti-oxidants, and 20 vitamins and minerals. Double-Yum!

Ingredients:
1 1/2 cups unsweetened almond milk
1 scoop protein powder
1 tablespoon goji berry powder
1 tablespoon maca
Optional: 3-4 ice cubes

Instructions:
Place all ingredients in a blender and blend for about 20 seconds or until smooth. Serve and feel nourished.

Espresso Bean Smoothie
Serves 1

Ingredients:
1 cup unsweetened almond milk
1 scoop protein powder
2 ounces espresso or strong coffee or 1 tablespoon granulated espresso powder
1 tablespoon maca
Optional: 3-4 ice cubes

Instructions:

Place all ingredients in a blender and blend for about 20 seconds or until smooth. Serve and feel nourished.

Chocolate Mint Protein Smoothie
Serves 1

Ingredients:
1 cup unsweetened almond milk
1 scoop protein powder
2 tablespoons raw cacao nibs
1/8 teaspoon peppermint extract
1 tablespoon maca
1 tablespoon raw cacao powder
1 handful spring mix lettuce or baby spinach
Optional:
3-4 ice cubes

Instructions:
Place all ingredients in a blender and blend for about 20 seconds or until smooth. Serve and feel nourished.

Chocolate Mousse That Loves 'Ya Back
Serves 1
Chocolate mousse in the traditional sense is out for me now. And by traditional I mean packed with sugar and heavy cream. The last time I tried some was a few years ago and I didn't feel so great afterwards. But I still love chocolate and I still adore that cloud-like texture of a mousse and guess what? I found something that approximates it, and it came about quite accidentally during the DDPYOGA Retreat Extravaganza at Riviera Maya-based El Dorado Resort and Spa. One morning before the workout session, I stood at the juice bar, ordering my usual mango and papaya-laden smoothie when I spied a bowl of avocados next to the blender. In my best fragmented Spanish, I asked the smoothie barista to add one. Why not? They were

back there for a reason...When he handed me the peach colored concoction, I realized I'd need a spoon to experience it. And believe me, it was love at first ultra-whipped bite. I devoured it, delighting in the knowledge that I was enjoying something so thoroughly that would not do me damage. And you KNOW when I got back to the states I had to try the avocado experiment in chocolate. Trust me, it works. This recipe is part dessert, part protein drink. But the important thing is, it's pure satisfaction: both physically and psychologically.

Ingredients:

1 ripe Haas avocado
1 cup unsweetened almond milk
1 scoop protein powder
1 tablespoon Coco Mojo (see glossary)
1 tablespoon raw cacao
1 teaspoon coconut palm sugar or 8 drops of stevia
1 tablespoon maca
* *Note: Have a bit of room temperature coffee, espresso, or water in case the mixture's too thick to blend properly. I usually add a tablespoon or two of espresso because it helps the texture and ups the rich flavor.*

Instructions:
Halve avocado and remove pit. Scoop out fruit with a spoon and place in a blender. Add milk and blend until smooth. Add remaining ingredients and blend until smooth. Add espresso or water if it's too thick and powders are not completely blending. Pour into a tumbler and enjoy with a spoon (you'll probably need to scrape the blender with rubber spatula).

Cleansing Classics

Vegetable Broth or Hot Juicing!

I can't really claim to be starting a trend with this one. A similar philosophy and recipe can be found in the 2004 best seller "French Women Don't Get Fat," which, I might add, had nothing to do with me becoming not-fat, but it's an interesting read. In the book, author Mireille Guiliano prescribed a "Magical Leek Soup" recipe, which one is to subsist on for about a 48-hour period for cleansing and weight-loss purposes.

I remember trying this weekend cleanse technique when the book first came out. Emotionally and spiritually, I was in no condition to undergo 58 minutes, let alone an entire weekend sans solid food. I think I ended up using the remaining leek broth as a boiling agent for an army sized pot of mashed potatoes. Aaahh, the days of eating ferociously. How I don't miss them.

Fast forward to a nippy, late September afternoon. I'm feeling sluggish, a little blue perhaps, as I mentally take note that is was 3 p.m. and I hadn't ingested all that many vegetables that day. As the wind howled a little louder, it became clear that it wasn't a day where a cool, tall glass of kale juice was going to suffice. Instead, I hightailed it to the vegetable drawer in the refrigerator for some organic kale. Into the stock pot I tossed it, along with five onions and an equal number of celery sticks. Filling the pot half-full with purified water, I brought it to a boil and shut the flame off. That's the secret to 'Hot Juicing.' Let the ingredients steep, not simmer to gently coax the essential elements and flavors out of the vegetables. Steeping time should be a minimum of two hours, four or five it you have the time. Since this is meant to be a cleansing drink, just as a glass of ginger-beet juice is, I added no oil, spices, or condiments. Its flavor? Clean and mild. Nothing arousing to the taste buds, but my body sure enjoyed it, and I drank it throughout the afternoon. There's plenty leftover for the week, and if I find myself tiring of my own version of magical broth, I'll simply freeze it.

This also makes fantastic base for rice. And like juicing, the ingredients can be tailored to your tastes, or whatever's hanging out in your veggie crisper.

Whole-Lemon Water

Drinking hot water with lemon squeezed into it is an age-old lose-the-bloat technique. But I've got an even better one: use the entire lemon as an ultimate cleansing tool. The difference between the juice of a lemon and the inclusion of its rind is vast. And your body will feel the difference, I assure you. It has more vitamins and nutrients than the juice itself. My first pitcher yielded significant changes, including a pronounced boost of energy and feeling of well-being. And some of the lemon's most beneficial properties got to work immediately on my body. I'll put it another way, don't drink this kind of lemon juice if you're doing a long car ride. You'll want to be no more than a hop, skip and Jump away from a rest room.

But back to the joys of the whole lemon: According to the website Healthy Food House, the benefits of ingesting the peel include the regulation of blood pressure, improved hygiene of the oral cavity, protection from fungal bacterial infections, and decreasing cholesterol levels. Slice a clean lemon, place in a pot of water and bring just to a boil. Steep for at least 30 minutes before drinking. It's best to drink it warm or room temperature. Don't be distressed if there's a slightly bitter taste at first, your palate will adjust. I get a lot of mileage out of one lemon. The pitcher I use isn't very big (about 10 ounces) so I resteep the slices throughout the day. If you travel to work, this is the perfect reason to dust off that unused thermos or invest in a new one. One final and important bit of advice: Because I'm utilizing the peel, I don't want to be steeping pesticides, so I splurge on organic lemons. It's worth the extra bit of cash.

Bragg's Apple Cider Vinegar Tonic

Hands down, the simplest recipe in the book. This was imparted to me by my wonderful nutritionist, Nancy Guberti, who recommends a glass of purified water and teaspoon of Bragg's Apple Cider Vinegar, preferably on an empty stomach. It cleanses the digestive track and helps with yeast and candida overgrowth on the stomach lining - a common disorder that effects just anyone who eats sugar and simple carbs on a regular basis. Though it sounds like a minor condition and most people 'afflicted' go about their day just fine, it can effect energy levels, interfere with nutrient absorption, and mental clarity.

Herbal tea

Herbal tea is something you should really consider adding to your beverage repertoire if it's not already a part of it. Herbal tea is gentle, comes in a variety of flavors based on their botanical base, and is perfect (and actually quite necessary) to drink after a heavy or fatty meal. Asian cultures have been doing it for centuries and it's because hot tea has a positive effect on the digestive system, unlike cold, icy drinks. Chinese and Ayurvedic medicine liken the digestive system as a fire that burns. The ingestion of cold food and drinks is literally akin to dousing that fire. If the idea of drinking hot liquids throughout the day is odd to you, start with a cup of tea a day and work up to 2 or 3. Even that will make a difference. Brewing:

Food & Wine editor Dana Corwin recently tweeted that the best way to make herbal tea is to simmer loose tea in a pot, NOT in a tea ball. After it simmers with the heat off for several minutes, pour tea through a strainer into a cup. Corwin says the tea needs its space while exuding its properties during the simmering process and tea balls don't cut it. If you don't use loose tea, simply add boiling water to a mug with a tea bag in it. Let steep for 3-4 minutes then remove the bag.

The Benefits of Hot Water

Yes, it's not just for jacuzzi-soaking. Hot water is great for your insides as well. About 15 years ago, I read Deepak Chopra's Ayurvedic-themed book on losing weight and better health called "Perfect Weight." It was full of sound, non gimmicky advice and therefore wasn't a best seller. And I read it at a time in my life when I simply wasn't able or ready to give up binge-eating. But I did take with me one piece of advice from his book: drink hot water. As hot as you can stand it. Hot water, said Chopra, cleanses the digestive track like nothing else, and since our body temperature is supposed to hover around 98 degrees, it just makes sense that sending down a liquid that's hot and not frigid would be helpful in the smooth operation of such an important and magnificent machine.

Soup's On!

Garbanzo Bean Soup
Serves 2
I nick-named this thick and hearty soup "Dinner on Deadline Soup" because I made it on a winter evening when I was behind the 8-ball but squeezed in a DDPYOGA workout anyway, which made my stomach rumble even more! Refusing to succumb to unhealthy quick fixes like fast food or frozen dinners, my eyes came upon a can of garbanzo beans (or chick peas as they're sometimes called) in the cupboard. I consider these mellow little lentils one of nature's most perfect and useful foods because they're low in fat and high in fiber and nutrients. I use garbanzos in everything from hummus, to baking bean-based chocolate cakes, to hearty soups like this one. All you need is a few ingredients and a food processor. Viola – a healthy meal in 30 minutes!

Ingredients:
1 can drained garbanzo beans
1 large clove garlic
3 tablespoons tomato paste
1 cup beef or vegetable stock
1 tablespoon dried thyme
Salt to taste

Instructions:
Preheat oven to 300. Place all ingredients in a food processor and blend until smooth. Bake in a covered crock for 30 minutes and serve. Finish with a drizzle of extra virgin olive oil. If you're feeling it, add some cooked brown rice, quinoa, or gluten-free pasta.

Henry's Chicken Stock (The Jewish Way)
Serves 6
This flavorful stock can be used as a delicious base to other soups, gravies, or sauces. It's also a great substitute for plain old water when making rice. Bill's late, great father, Henry, was a highly adept Jewish home cook. He used this recipe as a basis for the Jewish classic - chicken soup. It really is a salve for the soul:

Ingredients:
1 whole chicken, rinsed (approximately 5 pounds)
4 large carrots, peeled and quartered
4 large onions, peeled and quartered
4 large celery stalks, peeled and quartered
1 tablespoon fresh chopped dill
1/2 teaspoon black pepper
1/2 teaspoon kosher salt

Instructions:
Place chicken in a large stock pot covered with water. Bring to a boil on high heat. Boil chicken for five minutes. Fat and grey matter will come to top of pot. Turn heat down and skim the top of pot with a small strainer or fine-slotted spoon and discard. Turn heat back up until stock starts to slowly simmer. Add all other ingredients. Simmer on low heat covered for approximately an hour. Remove vegetables and chicken from broth. If you're desiring a classic pot of chicken soup, dice the vegetables and chicken meat and return to the pot with some cooked rice or noodles. If you just want clear stock, leave as is and repurpose the chicken meat and vegetables.

Vegan 'Cream' of Cauliflower Soup
Serves 4
What I love about this soup, aside from its velvety texture and subtle flavor, is I'm getting all the goodness of a cruciferous vegetable dose without the unpleasantness of chomping on cauliflower florets. I know they're good for me but they're not a favorite. This soup solves that dilemma. It's great as a snack, lunch, or a light dinner.

The recipe was born in part of me wanting to make vegan whipped cream out of coconut milk. For that, I needed two cans of coconut milk, refrigerated for two days so the cream would rise in a single, concentrated layer at the top. With the cream extracted, whipped, and safely entombed in Tupperware for when a craving strikes, I was left with more than two cups of perfectly good coconut water. It would have been fine in a smoothie, but my chilled bones were calling for soup. There were enough milky strands of coconut cream left in the water to make the soup just creamy enough to not taste like I was eating a liquidated head of cauliflower. But it wasn't fatty enough that I felt it wise to relegate myself to a tiny serving. Calorie-wise, it's the perfect middle-of-the-road soup.

The key here is texture. And I didn't have the patience to wield an immersion blender for the amount of time it would take to make the roughness of the cauliflower transmute to velvety smoothness, so I blended it in batches in a food processor. SO worth the effort. There's not much going on in terms of extra flavor notes with this recipe, which means you can have a field day with your spice and condiment cupboard. Paprika, cumin, and onion powder are all viable options, but I have to say that a drizzle of truffle oil is magic.

Ingredients:
1 head of cauliflower, rinsed and cut into chunks
2 cans of coconut water (with the fat strained and reserved for whipped cream) *
1/2 teaspoon salt
* You can also use a light coconut milk if you don't want to bother straining full-fat coconut milk. I do it this way because I use the coconut cream to make whipped cream (see dessert section). A tablespoon or two of coconut cream is great in smoothies.

Instructions:
In a medium stockpot or large saucepan, bring all ingredients to a boil. Cover and simmer on low heat for 20-30 minutes, until cauliflower is fork-tender. Let cool for a half-hour or so before pureeing. Puree in small batches – it's the best way to ensure the cauliflower properly breaks down to yield proper smoothness. If serving immediately, return to the pan and reheat on low heat, stirring occasionally so it doesn't burn or stick.

Root Vegetable Soup
Serves 6
I make a pot of this soup when I want to feel warm and grounded. There's something inherently stabilizing about root

vegetables and they're great slow-roasted, but there's nothing quite like a bowl of root vegetable soup.

Ingredients:

1 bunch scallions, washed and diced
2 medium onions, diced
4 large leeks, cleaned and chopped into 2-inch pieces
2 large turnips, washed and chopped into chunks
3 medium parsnips, peeled and chopped into pieces
2 large potatoes or 1 large yucca, peeled and cut in chunks
2 quarts of chicken or vegetable stock
Grapeseed or light olive oil for sauteing
1 tsp. sea salt
1 Tbs. fresh thyme
1 Tbs. fresh dill

In large stock pot, saute scallions and onions in olive oil over medium heat for 10 minutes. Use enough oil to thoroughly coat vegetables. After 10 minutes, turn heat to medium high and add remaining ingredients and bring to a boil. Turn heat to medium, cover tightly, and simmer for at least 30 minutes, until vegetables are fork-tender. Remove lid, turn heat off and let cool for half and hour before pureeing in batches in a food processor.

After soup is thoroughly pureed, add salt and spices. Heat on medium low heat for 10 minutes, stirring occasionally. Serve and drizzle with a bit of extra virgin olive oil. Like most soups, this freezes well. Place in small plastic storage containers and freeze for a night when you're too busy or tired to cook.

Avogelmeno
Serves 4
The first time I tried this at a Greek diner, I was smitten. It was chicken and rice soup elevated to a new level. That was thanks to the lemon juice...and of course, egg yolks! They turn thin stock into a golden, creamy bowl of comfort.

Ingredients:

5 cups Henry's Chicken Stock (see recipe)
1/3 cup white rice, uncooked
4 egg yolks (reserve whites for meringue or cauliflower mousse)
1/4 cup fresh lemon juice
1 tablespoon of lemon zest
1/2 teaspoon sea salt

Instructions:
Bring stock to a boil in a medium sauce pan. Add rice and let simmer, covered for 20 minutes until rice is cooked. Turn to low heat. Remove four ounces of stock and set aside to cool slightly. In a small mixing bowl, whisk eggs, lemon juice, and rind until smooth. Slowly add the cooled stock and whisk vigorously. When it's thoroughly blended, return lemon-egg mixture to the sauce pan and stir thoroughly. Heat for 10 minutes on low heat, stirring occasionally, until soup is thickened and ready to serve.

New England Clam Chowder
Serves 4-6
Bill invented this one afternoon after hearing me lament how I missed clam chowder. It was probably my favorite soup of all time and since it's so dairy heavy, was no longer compatible with my dairy-free, reformed way of eating. Oh I would have a cheat day every few months in the beginning, but the longer I ate dairy-free, the less hospitable my body became to dairy. Eventually it became no longer worth the price I'd pay in feeling lousy after eating a bowl of the cream-laden soup. In spite of Bill's talents in the kitchen, I was skeptical about a dairy-free version of New England Clam Chowder that actually tasted good. Heck, I was willing to settle for tasting OK. But this surpassed my expectations! I hope it will yours as well:

Ingredients:
3 medium-sized white potatoes, skinned and coarsely chopped
1 tablespoon light olive oil
1/4 pound of finely chopped bacon or any smoked meat you desire
1 small onion, finely chopped

2 cans chopped or minced clams, juice drained and set aside
1 small bottle of extra clam juice
1 tablespoon fresh finely chopped thyme
1/2 teaspoon black pepper

Instructions:
Boil potatoes in water until just soft (about 15 minutes). Drain.
Mash with a fork or potato masher and set aside. About half
of the potatoes should be creamy and pulverized, but there
should be some bits and chunks of potatoes. You don't want a
complete mash. In a medium stock pot, sauté chopped bacon
and onions over medium heat until onions are just translucent
(approximately 5 minutes). Turn heat down and slowly whisk
in all the clam juice (not clams). Gradually whisk potatoes into
mixture. Add pepper and thyme. If mixture seems too thick,
you may add extra clam juice. Add clams and gently simmer
for approximately 5 minutes, until thoroughly warmed. Stir
occasionally while warming.

Creamy Tomato Soup
Serves 4
One of the easiest dinners on the run ever. I invented this soup
one evening when I wanted something warm and filling but
not a big meal. Since I always have canned tomato products on
hand and usually have chevre in the refrigerator, I was in luck.
When I make this for people they're amazed it's so simple - and
that it has no cream in it.

Ingredients:
1 32-ounce can of crushed tomatoes or tomato puree
1 4-ounce log of chevre, room temperature if possible

Instructions:
Heat tomatoes in medium saucepan over medium heat until
sauce begins to simmer. Add chevre and whisk continually
until it's smooth and all the lumps are dissolved. Serve
immediately. Goes well with a gluten-free baguette!

Quick Pasta E Fagiole

Serves 6

Who doesn't love this hearty soup? It evokes grandmotherly memories, is warm and filling, and contrary to modern myth, doesn't take days, or even hours to make. Here's a quickie version that can render a pot of old-world Italian soup in under an hour:

Ingredients:
1/3 cup light olive oil or grapeseed oil
1 medium zucchini, washed and diced
1 carrot, peeled and diced
1 large or 2 medium onions, diced
2 celery stalks, diced
3 large or 4 medium cloves garlic, minced
* Note a food processor works wonders for the dicing
2 32-ounce cans of crushed tomatoes
1 quart chicken or vegetable stock
1 15-ounce can pink or pinto beans, drained
1 15-ounce can white beans or cannellini, drained
1 1/2 cups GF agnelli or soup pasta, dry
1 teaspoon salt
1 tablespoon dried oregano
2 tablespoons extra virgin olive oil
Grated Peccorino for garnish

Instructions:
In a large stock pot, sauté light olive oil with chopped vegetables over medium heat for 10 minutes, stirring occasionally. Add crushed tomatoes, stock, beans, and pasta and bring to a boil. Cook over medium heat for 8-9 minutes, until pasta is soft but firm. Turn off heat and add salt, oregano, and extra virgin olive oil. Stir thoroughly, cover, and let sit for 10 minutes. Serve and garnish with grated cheese.

New Year's Day Lentil Soup

Serves 6

One of the longstanding traditions in our family was pork and sauerkraut on New Year's Day. I'm not sure what the ritual was supposed to usher in, but in our house it was an unshakable cooking odor that seemed to seep into the molecular level of the carpeting and drapes and hover like a semi-hostile ghost for weeks. Nowadays, my New Year's Day Tradition is a little cleaner...in more ways than one. I still have days when I'm nothing but carnivorous, but the frequency is less. I've discovered it's just a natural change that occurred during the past three years as I've dropped 185 through clean eating (specifically no gluten or cow-dairy) and being physically engaged (DDPYOGA, long distance walking, weight-lifting). Oh yeah, and feeling with awareness. What, did you think it was all about calories and exercise? No one gets to where I was on the scale without doing some serious sprinting away from feelings, and if you're looking for similar freedom from bondage, you'd better learn to make friends with feeling what you're avoiding most, or it's gong to be a long and bumpy ride through the valley of dieting snake oil salesmen.

But back to the subject. I've still gotta eat. Heck, I still love it; I mean REALLY love it and always will, only now, I zero in on food that enhances everything: my mood, the way my vital organs function, and my metabolism. Firm rule of thumb: it's got to taste good or why bother. I spent too many years in purgatory pretending bone-dry 'oven fried' chicken was just as good as the real thing. No more of that. When I want fried chicken, I go to Hattie's. And when it's a cold, gloomy January day, I often want some version of lentil soup. There are endless varieties of them and not just because of the dozens of varieties of lentils out there. They adapt beautifully to any spice palate. Lentils are also astoundingly inexpensive, and loaded with nutrition. And when blended with a simple carb like rice or potatoes, equate to a complete protein...no meat or cheese necessary to round out the meal.

Here's a version I did on New Year's Day. To be honest, when I do soup, I just rummage through the spice cabinet and shake whatever strikes my fancy that day into the pot. For this batch it was something like paprika, onion salt, rosemary, and cayenne pepper. Soups are very forgiving and hard to screw up completely. If you're a novice, don't be afraid to play with flavors. You'll probably end up savoring the results.

Ingredients:
1 bag lentils (usually it's split orange lentils)*
2 large to medium onions, sliced or diced**
1 head garlic, cloves smashed
Olive or grapeseed oil for sautéing the vegetables
Two tablespoons of seasoning: whatever's in the cupboard.
Paprika, garlic or onion powder, thyme, sage, rosemary.
Whatever blend you choose should total about two tablespoons.
1/4 cup powdered chicken stock or 4 bouillon cubes

Note:
** If using whole lentils, like pinto beans or black-eyed peas,
you'll need to soak them in water overnight*
***You can add chopped carrots, celery, leeks to the onions and
garlic. No rules with this soup!*

Instructions:
Pour split lentils into a large stock pot and add about a quart
of purified drinking water. Let soak for two hours. Water will
absorb into the lentils. After two hours of soaking, place lentils
over medium heat and add more water until they're submerged
by about 3 inches. In a large frying pan, add chopped vegetables
and enough oil to coat them well. Sauté over medium heat until
at least soft and translucent. It's OK if some of them brown,
it enhances the soup's flavor. Set cooked vegetables aside as
lentils continue to cook. After about an hour, do a texture check
to see if lentil are soft enough to eat. They should somewhere
in between hard pellets and mush. A bit al dente, but with some
give. Once they're cooked to desired texture, add the bouillon,
spices, and vegetables and simmer on low heat for about 15
minutes.

As we all know, soup's better the next day, but you may want
to dig into this immediately. I served this version with a sticky-
wild rice blend, but you can go with potatoes or gluten-free
pasta. A little Peccorino cheese (a sheep's milk cheese that's
similar to Parmesan) sprinkled over each bowl makes it extra
Divine.

Condiments

Preserved Meyer Lemon

Preserved Meyer Lemons are the greatest thing to happen to cooking since salt. They add body and zest to pasta, chicken, and fish. Meyer lemons are smaller and sweeter than traditional lemons. This recipe lends itself to the distinctiveness of Meyer lemons, but traditional lemons work well also. The addition of preserved lemons absolutely MAKES Bill's crab pasta recipe, and is also good on steak. Once you try, you'll never go back to using the expensive (and not as good) store-bought preserved lemons.

Ingredients:
1 16-oz glass jar or mason jar
8 regular lemons or 12 Meyer lemons
1/2 cup salt
Extra virgin olive oil as needed

Instructions:
In a saucepan, blanche lemons (whole) for two minutes. Drain. When cool enough to handle, halve and squeeze approximately half the lemons into a glass bowl. Add 1 tsp. salt to the bottom of the glass jar. Other lemons should be cut into wedges, approximately 5 wedges per lemon. Insert lemon wedges into jar in layers to salt evenly, alternating lemon wedges and a teaspoon or two of salt until the jar is full. If this doesn't fill the jar, you can cut the rinds from the squeezed lemons and add as many as needed. Through a strainer, pour lemon juice into jar. Cover tightly. Let sit on counter out of the sunlight for four days, flipping the jar on opposite end each morning. On the fifth day, top off with extra virgin olive oil until jar is completely full, and rotate jar one more day. Refrigerate. Lemons will be ready for use in approximately a week. Lemons will keep six months or more, adding olive oil as needed to keep submerged.

Sugarless Cranberry Sauce a La Helen Gurley Brown

Cosmopolitan magazine…circa 1988. It's the last place I ever thought I'd find a usable recipe. But I did. And it was so simple, I committed it to memory in the confines of that sweat bath of a studio apartment I rented on the upper west side that summer. There's no sugar in this, which is amazing for a cranberry recipe. Use it any way you like: in yogurt, oatmeal, on ice cream, waffles. And of course, as a ruby-colored accompaniment to a Thanksgiving turkey dinner. No rules. Except one: don't under any circumstances leave the stove while this is simmering. You haven't really cleaned until you've cleaned molten cranberry sauce off a burner. I'm naming this concoction in honor of the woman who (on some level) must have given it the green light.

Ingredients:
1 bag fresh cranberries
1 can frozen grape juice concentrate (100% juice)

Instructions:
Place both ingredients in a sauce pan on medium heat and cover. Cook about 5-10 minutes, or until it begins to simmer. Uncover and turn heat to medium-low. Let simmer for about 30 minutes, stirring occasionally. Let cool before serving or storing. Keeps for several weeks in the refrigerator. Months if frozen.

Olive Tapenade
I detested olives when I was a child...couldn't even look at them. Now, I adore all varieties: out of the jar, in a mezze platter, as a pizza topping, in pasta dishes as an accent. I don't eat great quantities of olives, and they're probably not meant for that because of their saltiness. Besides their famous pairing with the Martini, they're fantastic with eggs, burgers, and chicken dishes. When my friend Jenny (who grew up in Puerto Rico) served me a bowl of rice and beans bejeweled with sliced green olives, I realized they work well with just about anything...a few exceptions being ice cream sundaes and buttercream frosting. Eventually I stumbled upon the phenomenon known as tapenade, probably while wandering through a gourmet specialty shop back when I lived in New York City. It was good, but pricey, which led me to my kitchen food processor to see if I could do it better. Guess what? I did. And I'm happy to share the results.

There are no hard and fast rules with homemade olive tapenade. I tend to use equal parts black and green olives (pimentos are optional, but pitted olives are an imperative). I accent it with either hot or sweet peppers depending on what's in the pantry and my mood. Also crucial is extra virgin olive oil – it's the same principal as using decent wine when cooking, plus the extra virgin is healthier and the emerald color makes for a more enticing spread. Other than that, it's your comfort level where raw garlic is concerned and a few dashes of Oregano and Rosemary if you have it. If you have fresh leaves available, even better. Another reason to try tapenade: olives are acidic by nature and aid in digestion, and a spoonful of this or two constitutes a few olives. It's one of the most flavorful and healthy accents you can give food, and a nice option besides butter or cream to jazz up a dish. All you need is a food processor and a little time.

Ingredients:
1 32-ounce jar green olives with pimentos, drained
2 16-ounce cans black olives, drained
1 16-ounce jar of peppers (hot or sweet)
1 tablespoon each dried Rosemary and Oregano (if you have fresh, ratio can be higher….season to taste)
4-9 fresh garlic cloves (season to taste)
Extra virgin olive oil

Place olives, peppers, herbs, and garlic in mixing bowl. You won't be able to pulse contents in one shot, so add as much to the food processor as can be comfortably pulsed and pulse until mixture turns almost granular, but still has rough edges…. you don't want mush. Remove in batches and place in another mixing bowl. Repeat until all olive mixture is blended. In mixing bowl filled with chopped olive mixture, drizzle enough olive oil to make an emulsified paste. It shouldn't be like soup, but a little sloshy and wet. Blend thoroughly with wooden spoon or rubber spatula and store in plastic containers or glass jars. Keeps for a few months in the refrigerator, tightly covered (preferably in a glass jar). Place in the back of the fridge if storing for a few months – do not freeze.

Power Pesto
Makes about 2 cups
A few months ago I discovered I actually kind of dig roasted Brussels sprouts. If they're halved and drizzled in olive oil, sprinkled with a bit of good salt then baked until just crisp (not charred) they possess a genuine appeal. One day, as I noticed a Tupperware container full of leftover roasted Brussels in the fridge, it got me thinking. Maybe because it's spring and greens are everywhere but I but I had a pesto-pasta craving and the wheels started turning. Why couldn't a food processor shred the Brussels to bits so innocuous they'd blend perfectly into a pesto sauce while simultaneously providing all those good things to my body Brussels are known for?

There was one way to find out, and the result is the recipe below. I tried it. I loved it. And I really couldn't tell I was downing a batch of Brussels sprouts. They key is roasting. It adds a depth of flavor that you can't get from boiled or raw. Takes a little time, but well worth it. Don't get too hung up on exact amounts in a pesto recipe. A lot of it is to taste. If you like it garlicky, or more cheesey, adjust accordingly. Ditto for the olive oil. If you're trying to stretch it out or simply prefer it more runny vs. chunky, use a heavy hand when pouring the oil. The point is to enjoy, and serve over gluten-free pasta or spread on a gluten-free bagel or baguette. Making a creation that used to be a no-no for me into a clean delight is pure, unmitigated fun.

Ingredients:
1 1/2 to 2 cups roasted Brussels Sprouts, room temperature
1 cup or more of fresh basil leaves
1/4 cup Peccorino cheese
1/2 to 1 cup extra virgin olive oil
3-6 cloves garlic
Blend all ingredients in a food processor until a smooth paste is formed. Serve immediately over hot pasta or toasted bread.

Spinach Pesto
Makes about 2 cups

Disguising the appearance and texture of a vegetable is the underlying point of a recipe like this if you're not especially fond of little green fronds. Believe me, I couldn't have dropped 180 pounds and kept it off for nearly five years if I didn't become more amenable to subsisting on more cauliflower, cabbage, kale, and spinach…I'm much more cooperative than I was a decade ago…but I still need coaxing. Thankfully, the January issue of O magazine gave me a brilliant idea and I ran with it: Spinach Pesto.

That's pesto as in, no basil, ALL SPINACH. You'd think that as a passionate home cook, healthy eater, and recipe developer, this would have occurred to me long ago. But no matter, I had a 10-ounce tub of fresh spinach in my crisper drawer just waiting

for a purpose. I loosely followed the O magazine guideline and came up with this emerald-colored and surprisingly flavorful sauce, which I paired with mung bean pasta. I've been having a love affair with the simple, pale-colored mung lately: Our New Year's Day pancakes were made with a gluten-free flour blend that included mung flour, coconut flour, and blue cornmeal, and two days ago I made a massive pot of mung bean soup. Mung pasta is a little on the chewy side, but its upsides are many, including the fact that it's gluten-free, heavy on the protein and fiber, and rich in iron, while being light on sugars and simple carbs. Double win!

Ingredients:
1 10-ounce tub prewashed baby spinach
4 cloves garlic, peeled
1/2 cup of grated Peccorino cheese (made from sheep's milk)
1/4 cup of lemon juice
About a cup of extra virgin olive oil (this amount can vary, what you want is enough oil to make a slightly liquidy paste; something that will emulsify easily over pasta)

Instructions:

In a food processor, blend ingredients together and pulse until smooth. If your food processor is medium-sized like mine, you'll have to do the pesto in several batches. Don't be alarmed at the mountain of spinach…it chops down to nothing in no time. When first batch is done (you don't want to overcrowd the food processor), scrape pesto into a small mixing bowl and start second batch. Serve immediately over pasta and refrigerate any excess. I recommend storing in an airtight container, where it will keep for a few weeks. This is also fantastic on toast or a toasted bagel.

Now isn't THAT a fabulous way to get the greens?

Herbs...They Look Nice, But What Do I Do With 'Em?

I generally ascribe to the are no (or very few) rules when it comes to using spices and herbs, especially fresh ones. If Bill has come home with a spring of soft Rosemary from the market, I make the most of its finite fragrance and texture. One time I tore off about 2 tablespoons of fresh rosemary needles and placed them in a coffee bean grinder and blended them into a gritty powder. That was all it took to bring a batch of crispy polenta squares to an elevated level that wowed the dinner guests (and us).

Don't be skittish about investing in fresh herbs. They really don't cost a fortune, and if you end up using only a fraction of that Rosemary sprig for your chicken recipe, guess what? You can make a sumptuous pot of herbal tea with what remains. If you haven't tried savory teas, they are wonderful. And healthy. Simply throw in a bunch of herbs (stems and all) into a kettle or medium-sized saucepan and fill with water. Bring to just under a boil, shut heat off, and let steep for at least an hour, covered. Discard leaves and imbibe some of Mother Nature's most wonderful gifts.

Vegetables Under The Radar

Going clean four years ago has meant many things. There's no one way to define how I dropped 185 pounds without dieting or surgery. It was a combination of giving up certain things while taking others on. Gone was the pattern of binge-eating when I was having a bad day…or just falling into it out of habit. It docs become a habit if repeated often enough. Next to go were gluten and cow dairy. But I took habits on, like long-distance walking, DDPYOGA, and more eating more produce. Fruit was easy, but vegetables were a challenge. Greens and I don't exactly exude an intense chemistry, but I want to feel better and keep the weight off. I can't say that I ever felt lousy after eating vegetables the way I've felt lousy after overloading on potato chips and clam dip or a bucket of fried chicken. The problem I have with vegetables isn't in their nutritional merit but rather with taste and texture. But there arc ways to be creative. I LOVE discovering ways to eat healthy green vegetables while having little or no cognizance that I'm doing so.

Broccoli-Chevre Bake
Serves 4
One night, I decided to see how deftly I could slide broccoli under the taste bud radar and am happy to say, I DID IT! Even Chef Bill, who borderline dislikes broccoli couldn't stop eating this, so it's a ringing endorsement.
And it was easy. All that's required is a bag of frozen broccoli, a log of chevre, olive oil, preserved Meyer lemons (or half a lemon) and a food processor. That's it for a carb-free dinner or delicious vegetable side dish. Because the chevre and broccoli emulsify together during the baking process, this doesn't have as much of a sharp tang as, say, chevre would right out of the fridge. Here's to dining on cruciferous veggies…with pleasure:

Ingredients:
1 two-pound bag of broccoli florets
thawed
1 11-ounce log of chevre (goat cheese)
Extra virgin olive oil
2 Tablespoons preserved Meyer lemon or 2 Tablespoons lemon

juice

Optional: whip 2 or 3 eggs into the mixture for a fluffier texture and more protein. I've tried both ways and prefer the casserole without eggs because it lends a more intense, cheesy flavor.

Instructions:
Preheat oven to 325. In a food processor, blend some of the florets with a few sliced medallions of chevre in batches. It may be necessary to place already-minced broccoli in a bowl so the entire batch is evenly minced. As food processor is running, drizzle enough olive oil into the mixture to emulsify it. Consistency should be a thick paste, not liquidy. Spray a covered casserole dish with cooking spray and spoon broccoli-chevre mixture into the casserole. Bake for 15 minutes covered, and 15 minutes uncovered. If casserole feels dry when served, drizzle a bit more olive oil on top.

Cauliflower Hash
Serves 2
This absolutely stands up to the flavor of potato hash. The texture's a little different but it's crisp and delicious. It goes well with sunny-side up eggs, or as a side dish at dinner

Ingredients:
1 head of cauliflower (orange is my favorite)
1 medium onion
1 teaspoon salt
Grapeseed or light olive oil for frying

Instructions:
Chop stalks off of the cauliflower so that mostly the florets remain. Process florets in a food processor until they resemble a coarse sand. Depending on the size of your food processor, this may have to be done in batches. Place ground cauliflower in a mixing bowl, then process onion and add to the cauliflower. Mix the two together thoroughly and add salt.

In a cast iron or non-stick skillet, heat about a quarter-inch of oil on medium high heat for 2 minutes, then add cauliflower hash. After 5 minutes, reduce to medium heat and continue cooking until crisp, stirring occasionally so it's evenly cooked.

Zucchini Hash Browns
Serves 2
I love this as an alternative to potato hash browns. It's another way to get more greens into my life. I often have this with eggs in the morning or as a dinner side-dish.

Ingredients:
1 large or two medium zucchini
1 clove garlic
1/2 teaspoon sea salt
Light olive oil or grape seed oil for frying

Instructions:
Grate zucchini and garlic on a cheese grater using the largest holes for the zucchini and small or medium holes for garlic. Place grated zucchini in a small mixing bowl and mix the garlic in thoroughly. Sprinkle salt in and mix some more. In a non-stick or cast-iron skillet, heat about 1/4 cup of oil over medium high heat until oil begins to shimmer. Drop zucchini onto oil in 1/3-cup portions, flatten so they're pancake-like and fry about 3-4 minutes on each side. Zucchini pancakes may be placed in warm oven until the entire batch is made. Serve immediately.

Cauliflower Mousse
Serves 4
This is simple and spectacular! The texture is a cross between mousse and flan. It's so creamy and light - and there are no no-no's in the ingredients, so enjoy with abandon - it's good for you! And yes, it really is cauliflower.

Ingredients:
1 head cauliflower
1 cup chicken or vegetable stock
2 eggs
2 egg whites

1/4 cup So Delicious Barista Style Coffee Creamer
1 teaspoon sea salt

Instructions:
Preheat oven to 325. Rinse cauliflower and cut florets off of the stalks. Heat the chicken stock in a medium saucepan on high till boiling. Add florets, reduce heat to medium, and simmer covered for 15 minutes or until fork-tender. Drain all but a few tablespoons of the stock. Let florets cool uncovered for 10 minutes. In a food processor, blend florets with remaining ingredients until smooth. Spray a 8x8 brownie baking pan with non-stick spray and scrape cauliflower mixture into it. Bake for 25 minutes or until the center is solid to the touch. Cut into squares and serve immediately. This dish also works baked in individual custard ramekins, in which baking time would be cut back to 15 minutes.

Caramelized Fennel
Serves 1
I don't have a heck of a lot of life experience with fennel but discovered how good it is after visiting The Village Pizzeria in Galway, N.Y. The owner, Sandy Foster, makes an annual research visits to Italy and put caramelized fennel on her menu years ago. It's both savory and slightly sweet with licorice undertones. I love it as a side dish or with...you guessed it - eggs!

Ingredients:
1 large fennel bulb
salt to taste
Grapeseed or light olive oil for frying

Instructions: Preheat oven to 330. Slice the bulbous part of the fennel into thin rings. Leave the stalks and fronds aside or save them for making vegetable stock. Place fennel rings in a shallow baking dish and drizzle with enough oil to coat them well, massaging them a bit so oil is distributed. Bake fennel for 20-30 minutes, until smaller pieces are just crisp. Serve immediately.

Eggplant Latkes
Serves 4
These totally satisfy my fried food cravings, while keeping me out of the realm of potato chips, French fries, and fried chicken.

Ingredients:
1 large eggplant, cut in half lengthwise
2 tablespoons rice flour (tapioca or chick pea works also)
3 teaspoons Zataar (a Middle Eastern seasoning made with sumac and sesame seeds)
Salt to taste
Grapeseed oil (perfect for frying because of its high smoking point. If you don't have any, use light olive oil, not extra virgin)

Instructions:
Preheat oven to 300. Spray baking sheet with non-stick cooking spray and place eggplant face down. Bake at 300 for 30 minutes and turn oven off. Leave eggplant in an let cool for 15 minutes. When eggplant has become cool enough to touch, scoop out the eggplant's flesh with a fork into a mixing bowl. To get it all, use a knife to scrape at the end. Add flour and Zataar and mix thoroughly with a fork. Heat oil in a frying pan over medium to medium high heat. Use enough oil to cover bottom of pan. Drop eggplant mixture by the spoonful, making tiny pancakes (a bit bigger than a silver dollar). Fry for about 5-7 minutes on each side or until crisp. Flip and repeat. Transfer to plate, sprinkle with salt and serve immediately!

Starches

Yes, starches. Many people automatically assume that when I say I'm gluten-free that means I'm carb-free. Hardly! I attribute the mix up to my dramatic loss and the assumption that one must be carb-free in order to get rid of weight and keep it off. I eat carbs in moderation and some of the best ones on the planet are naturally gluten-free and ones you already enjoy.

Rosemary Polenta
Serves 4-6

Ingredients:
1 quart (4 cups) water
2 cups coarse yellow corn meal
2 teaspoons salt
2 tablespoons butter or extra virgin olive oil
1 cup hot water
2 tablespoons fresh rosemary, finely chopped or run through a coffee bean grinder* or small food processor. *This will effect the flavor of your bean grinder, so either wash thoroughly afterwards or do what I do: keep a bean grinder strictly for whirring fresh herbs!

Instructions:
Bring the water to a boil in a medium sauce pan. Using a wire whisk, sprinkle corn meal into the salted water, stirring constantly. Turn heat back to low and simmer covered for about 2 minutes, stirring occasionally and adding small increments of hot water if polenta becomes too stiff. Polenta should be a very thick liquid consistency, not solid or pasty. Turn off heat and add butter or oil. Preheat oven to 325. Spray or oil a 9x13 brownie pan generously and pour polenta in. Bake for 25 minutes or until solid. Serve immediately with butter or extra virgin olive oil. Great as an appetizer. Pairs well with chicken, lentil soups, or with morning eggs.

Crab Cappelini

Serves 2

Chef Bill made this for me early on in our courtship. I was already smitten with him, and this only sealed the deal. Up until that moment, I had only known pasta either drenched in Marinara sauce, Alfredo's or pungent pestos. Never had I experienced such delicate and intriguing flavor combinations as the gentleness of the crab overlaid with preserved lemons and just enough kick from the siracha.

Ingredients:

8 ounces of gluten-free thin spaghetti or cappelini
1/2 pound of lump crab meat, chopped
2 shallots, finely chopped
1 tablespoon Siracha
3 wedges of preserved lemons, finely chopped
2 tablespoons fresh parsley, finely chopped
1/3 cup extra virgin olive oil
1/2 stick unsalted butter, softened

Instructions:
Boil the pasta for 8 minutes or to your desired al-dente-ness. While pasta is cooking, sauté shallot in olive oil at medium heat. Cook to glassine, do not brown. Lower the heat and gently add crab and butter. Let cook until crab is warm and butter is melted. Add chopped lemons and siracha. Strain pasta and toss with crab mixture and parsley. Serve onto plates using tongs or pasta claw, making all is coated evenly. Chef's note: cheese garnish for this dish is not recommended. Let the delicate flavors of the crab and lemon do their thing. If you're a fan of heat, increase the amount of Siracha.

Lobster Risotto

Serves 6

This dish is luxuriously comforting, and you'll feel as though you've treated yourself to dinner at a high-end seafood house. If you have a shellfish allergy, or are vegan, substitute something delicious of your choice as an add-on: sauteed mushrooms, caramelized onions, a cup of your favorite shredded cheese all work fantastically.

Risotto is a short-grain Italian rice that can't just be dumped in simmering water and left for 20 minutes. Constant stirring is required, making it a time-consuming event, but at the same time, the process is simple and meditative.

Ingredients:
Six servings of Risotto (prepared according to box instructions, using seafood or vegetable broth as a base)
1 pound of lobster meat, pulled into chunks
Salt to taste
Butter for garnish

Instructions:
After risotto is prepared, let stand covered in the pot on the stove (no heat). Process the lobster meat in batches in a food processor. It should be finely shredded, almost paste-like. Turn a low flame under the Risotto and transfer lobster meat to the pot and mix thoroughly. If risotto becomes too thick and chunky, add small amounts of hot water or stock until it's creamy enough to fall off a turned spoon. Heat on low for another 5 minutes until mixture is thoroughly warmed. Garnish with butter and serve immediately.
* Note: If there are leftovers, do not reheat them on the stove. Use a covered casserole dish or crock - it will come back beautifully.

Tagliatelle with Garlic "Cream" Sauce
Serves 4
This amazing and unique recipe was inspired by Jim Rua and Andrew Plummer of the Albany landmark, Cafe Capriccio. The foundation of the original recipe called for lots of heavy cream. No can do anymore. Chef Bill made the recipe over and it comes darned close - but no dairy cramps!

Ingredients:
2 heads garlic, cloves peeled
1 bottle dry white wine (750 ml)
1 quart chicken stock
1 quart So Delicious Barista
Style Coffee Creamer
2 tablespoons cornstarch
2 tablespoons butter, softened
Fresh, chopped rosemary for
garnish
1 12-ounce box of GF
tagliatelle or fettuccine

Instructions: Place garlic
and wine in large saucepan and simmer uncovered at low to
medium heat until wine is evaporated, keeping watch that garlic
doesn't burn (it will probably brown though). Do NOT continue
cooking after liquid is evaporated. After wine is evaporated,
add chicken broth and simmer on low to medium heat until
until broth is evaporated. Mix cornstarch and softened butter
into a paste. Pulverize the garlic in the saucepan with a potato
masher or through a ricer. Add the creamer and whisk together
with garlic. Once this is simmering, add the softened butter and
cornstarch paste. Whisk continuously until thickened. Cover
and turn off heat.

Meanwhile, in a large stock pot, boil pasta with a splash of
oil and cook for 8 minutes, or until al dente, not super-soft.
Stir constantly in the beginning, making sure pasta strands
separate. Drain and place on serving plates or large pasta bowls.
Immediately ladle cream sauce over pasta. Sprinkle with fresh
rosemary.

Spaghetti Bolognese
Serves 4

Ingredients:
1 Bolognese Sauce A La Chef Bill recipe (see recipe)
1 box of gluten-free spaghetti

Instructions:
Heat Bolognese sauce on low heat, covered, while pasta is cooking. Bring stockpot of water to a boil. Add a splash of oil and then a box of gluten-free spaghetti and cook for 8 minutes. Stir constantly in the beginning, making sure pasta strands separate. Drain and place on serving plates or large pasta bowls. Immediately ladle Bolognese sauce over pasta. Sprinkle with peccorino cheese.

Chef Bill's Greek-Style Potatoes Lyonnaise
Serves 4-6
Lyonnaise potatoes are a little bit of work, but so worth it because of the firm, yet velvety texture yielded by boiling them prior to baking. These are a Greek delicacy so don't skimp on the fresh oregano!

Ingredients:
Approximately 2 pounds miniature fingerling or fancy potatoes, washed, skins-on
1 lemon, halved and juiced, rinds set aside
1/4 cup extra virgin olive oil
2 tablespoons chopped fresh oregano
1 teaspoon Kosher salt
1/2 teaspoon black pepper

Instructions:
Place potatoes and lemon rinds in large stock pot and cover with water. Bring to a boil over high heat and boil for 15 minutes, or till al dente (not completely soft). Drain gently and completely, patting dry with towels if necessary. Preheat oven to 275. Toss potatoes gently with spices, lemon juice, and oil in a large mixing bowl. Transfer potatoes to a baking sheet or roasting pan. Cook at 275 for 1 hour. Serve immediately.

Quinoa Tabouli
Serves 2
Tabouli is a traditional Middle Eastern salad of chopped vegetables and bulgar wheat. It's one of my favorite salads because of its crisp texture and fresh flavors. No need to give it

up though, just use quinoa instead of bulgar wheat.

Ingredients:
2 cups cooked quinoa, chilled
1 large carrot, minced or food processed
1/4 cup chopped olives or 1/4 cup olive tapenade (see recipe)
1 small onion, diced
1/3 cup halved cherry tomatoes
1/2 cucumber, coarsely chopped
1/2 fresh chopped herbs in any combination (mint, parsley, oregano)
Juice of 1 lemon
1/2 cup extra virgin olive oil
Salt and pepper to taste

Instructions: Remove quinoa from refrigerator and add to a medium-sized mixing bowl. Add all other ingredients, mix thoroughly, and chill for at least an hour or overnight. Serve chilled or at room temperature.

Basmati Rice
Serves 4
Sometimes I'll make a batch of rice and store it in the refrigerator for a ready-made side dish or as the answer to a carb craving when I'm food combining. Basmati rice is a nutritious long-grain rice from South Asia with a medium glycemic index, making it more suitable for diabetics than some other grains and white-flour products.

Ingredients:
1 quart chicken or vegetable stock
2 cups basmati rice
1 teaspoon sea salt
2 tablespoons olive oil
* If serving with chicken add 1 teaspoon sage. If serving with fish, add 1 teaspoon lemon zest.

Bring stock to a boil in medium saucepan. Add rice, salt, and oil and stir thoroughly. Cover and simmer 20 minutes over medium heat. Turn heat off and let stand for 10 minutes before adding the optional flavorings of sage or lemon zest. Fluff with a fork before serving. Optional: add a pat of butter to rice pot and fluff to 'finish' with a nice gloss.

Football Cornbread
Makes 1 pan of cornbread
This recipe is adapted from a cornbread recipe on the Peas and Crayons blog, which was adapted from Food.com. I found Peas and Crayons' recipe to be quite appealing, doubled it for the Football crowd, and tinkered with the flours and milk.

Ingredients:
1 2/3 cup corn flour
2/3 cup white rice flour
1 cup mung bean flour
1 1/4 cup corn meal, stone ground
3 tablespoons baking powder
1 teaspoon salt
1/2 cup coconut palm sugar
1 stick of butter, softened
3 eggs at room temperature
1 cup So Delicious unsweetened coconut milk
2 tablespoons coconut oil

Instructions: Preheat oven to 350. Sift all dry ingredients (excluding sugar) together in a large mixing bowl. In a smaller bowl, cream butter into the coconut palm sugar, then add to dry ingredients and blend. Add eggs, one at a time until blended in. Heat milk and oil in a small saucepan until just lukewarm and oil melts. Add to the rest of the ingredients and whisk. Spray a 9x13 glass pan with cooking spray and scrape batter into pan, spreading evenly. Bake for 20-25 minutes. Center should feel solid to the touch, you don't want these over baked or they'll be sandy. Cut in squares and

serve warm with butter.
Henry's Caramelized Corn
Serves 2
Another favorite passed down from Bill's father, who loved
fresh corn in the summer...and not just the boiled variety.

Ingredients:
2-3 ears of corn, peeled
2-3 tablespoons butter or Earth Balance
Salt to taste

Instructions:
With a large serrated knife, carefully slice corn off the cobs. In
a skillet (preferably cast iron) melt butter. When it's bubbling,
add the corn and turn heat to medium high. Saute for five
minutes then move kernels around so corn gets evenly browned.
Cook for another five minutes, sprinkle with salt, if desired, and
serve.

The Classics: New and Oh So Improved

Remodeled Eggplant Parm
Serves 2

Chef Bill invented this delightful dinner one night in response to a craving. It's a cleaned up version of one of my favorites: Eggplant Parm. I was going to christen it Eggplant Pecc, but it just didn't have the proper ring. This dish may look elaborate and involved, but I assure you, it's very do-able. The crux of it involves dredging eggplant slices in gluten-free bread crumbs and then baking them until crisp. The slices are then layered in a baking dish with layers of a Bolognese-style meat sauce and topped with slices of Manchego cheese, a sheep's milk cheese. The result is positively delicious and no yucky, heavy feeling afterward.

Ingredients:
1 medium eggplant
1 cup (possibly more) of gluten-free bread crumbs
Grapeseed or light olive oil for baking eggplant
Chevre soft goat cheese (optional)
About 1/4 cup grated Peccorino cheese

Instructions:
Slice 1 medium eggplant into quarter-inch thick slices. Lay slices onto a sheet of paper towels to let water from the eggplant absorb. Let sit on paper towels for five minutes, then flip slices onto a new sheet of dry paper towels. Preheat oven to 400. Pour bread crumbs into a shallow dish and press eggplant slices firmly on each side, so slice is lightly coated. Place slices onto well oiled baking sheet. Bake 7-10 minutes. Flip with tongs, and bake another 7 minutes until crispy and golden. Remove from oven and set aside.

In an oven-proof ramekin, coat bottom generously with Bolognese sauce (see recipe) or marinara sauce. Layer in eggplant slices, each slice overlapping one another by about a
88

third. Add another layer of sauce over first layer of eggplant and cover with grated Manchego cheese. Follow with another layer of eggplant, sauce, and cheese. There should be three layers total. End with a generous layer of Manchego and Peccorino. Bake for 10 to 12 minutes until cheese is bubbling. * Optional: for a more creamy, lasagna-like dish, include dots of chevre in each layer, excluding the top layer.

Bolognese Sauce A La Chef Bill
Makes a large pot of sauce
Bolognese is a thick, hearty meat sauce named after Bologna, the city in northern Italy known for giving birth to beloved classic dishes such as ravioli and lasagna.

Ingredients:
Four large cloves of garlic or as desired, finely chopped
3 carrots, chopped
2 medium onions, chopped
1 pound organic ground beef
1 pound lean ground pork
2 32-ounce cans of diced tomatoes (Tutto Rosso or Hunt's)
1 32-ounce can of tomato sauce
1/2 cup red wine
1/2 cup beef stock
1 small can tomato paste to thicken if needed
3 tablespoons fresh oregano
2 tablespoons fresh thyme
1/2 teaspoon white pepper
1/2 cup extra virgin olive oil
1/2 teaspoon Kosher salt

In a large saute pan, sauté beef and pork until brown. Strain excess fat and blot meat. Transfer to a medium stockpot. Add half the olive oil to sauté pan. Sauté carrots and onions until onions are transluscent, not browned. Add garlic under low heat and sauté another minute. Add mixture to beef in stock pot.

Add cans of tomatoes and heat to simmer and then turn down to a low simmer. Add wine, stock, remaining oil and spices and simmer with cover ajar on very low heat, stirring occasionally for about an hour and 15 minutes. Add tomato paste to thicken if necessary.

Chef Bill's No-Carb Meatloaf
Pure protein - Pure comfort!

Ingredients:
1 pound lean, organic ground beef
1 pound lean, organic ground pork (optional, may use all beef)
Approximately 1/2 pound chopped cremini (baby bella) mushrooms (or your favorite)
2 eggs, well-beaten
1 small onion, finely chopped
1 teaspoon Worcestershire sauce
1 teaspoon sea salt
1/2 teaspoon black pepper
3 tablespoons finely chopped parsley
Olive or grapeseed oil for frying

Instructions: Preheat oven to 350. In a medium saucepan, sauté the mushrooms and cook until just before browned. Set aside in mixing bowl. Heat more oil over medium heat and sauté the onion until translucent, not browned. In a large mixing bowl, add ground beef and pork and knead together thoroughly. Add eggs and knead thoroughly. Pulverize cooked mushrooms in a food processor and let cool for five minutes before adding to meat mixture. Do not add them while piping hot. Mix well and add remaining ingredients and knead well. Spray a loaf pan with cooking spray. Place meat mixture in the pan and form gently, pushing sides down so center rises up like a slight crown. Bake for about an hour or until a meat thermometer reaches 160 (for ground beef and pork).

Italian Meatballs
Serves 6
Good enough to eat on their own. Of course, they're fantastic

with a side of spaghetti, but I love these flavor-packed meatballs sliced in half and sauteed till slightly crisp on one side and served with a side of spinach for a carb-free dinner.

Ingredients:
1 pound at least 90% lean organic ground beef
1 pound lean Italian sausage (sweet or hot depending on preferencc) *
3 slices high quality gluten-free white bread such as Udi's, food processed into crumbs
1/2 cup grated peccorino
2 eggs, well beaten
1/2 cup grated peccorino
2 eggs, extremcly well beaten
1/4 cup fresh chopped parsley
4 ounces tomato paste
1/2 teaspoon kosher salt
1/2 teaspoon black pepper

* Turkey sausage works as a substitute

Instructions:
Preheat oven to 350. In a large mixing bowl, combine and blend together all ingredients, forming a big ball. Using a 1/3 cup measure or a large ice cream scooper, uniformly shape balls of equal size. On a well oiled (light olive oil or grapeseed oil) bakc for approximately 14 minutes, then turn with tongs and bake for another 14 minutes. A quick-read thermometer should be 160.

Football Chili
Makes 1 large pot
In essence: this makes a big, delicious pot of chili, so either invite guests to help you enjoy it or allocate some freezer space for the leftovers. Using dried beans is more cost effective (and less can wasteful) and it also makes for firmer beans that don't

turn mushy after a few days.

Ingredients:
1 bag each of Great Northern White Beans, Pinto Beans and Black-Eyed Peas
2 teaspoons baking soda
2 32-ounce cans diced tomatoes
2 32-ounce cans tomato puree or crushed tomatoes
3 large onions, chopped
3 cloves garlic, chopped
1 3/4 pounds organic ground beef (or a combination of chicken, turkey or pork...your preference)
1 can dark beer
1 cup beef stock
4 tablespoons chili powder
2 tablespoons cumin
1 tablespoon coriander
1 tablespoon thyme
1 tablespoon cocoa powder
1 to 3 tablespoons Frank's Hot Sauce (preference)

Instructions: Empty beans into a large stock pot and cover with water, making sure the beans are submerged by at least 3 inches of water. Soak overnight with 1 Tbs. baking powder. It may be necessary to add more water the next day. Beans should be softened enough to bite into. When soft enough, drain water off the beans. Add all tomatoes, beef stock, and beer and heat over medium heat until simmering. In a large saute pan, saute beef until cooked. Drain well and add to stockpot. Saute chopped onions and chopped garlic in 1 Tbs. olive oil until onions are glassine, not browned. Add to stockpot, as well as all remaining ingredients. Stir and simmer at low heat for a minimum of 45 minutes. Chili can be thickened if desired by adding tomato paste; and thinned if desired by adding beef stock. Salt to taste.

Buffalo Shrimp
Serves 4
Chef Bill made these for me on a cold January afternoon when

he sensed I needed cheering up.   It was one of those 'one gray frigid day too many' scenarios and I was HUNGRY. I heard him bustling pots and pans around in the kitchen and knew he was up to something. Ten minutes later, he pranced into the study with a small plate of orange, glistening shrimp over baby greens. The shrimp were juicy and slightly crisp from the rice coating. The hot sauce elevated the ordinary to a new level. Suffice it to say it was a sizzling little snack that made my day.

Ingredients:
1 pound 21-25 fresh shrimp, peeled and deveined
1/2 cup rice flour
1/2 teaspoon black pepper
1/2 teaspoon sea salt
Light olive or grapeseed oil for frying
1/3 cup Frank's Hot Sauce
1/4 stick melted, unsalted butter

Instructions: Heat oil in cast iron skillet or wok for frying to approximately 350 degrees. Whisk salt and pepper into rice flour. In a pie plate or in a plastic, toss shrimp to coat evenly with flour mixture. Put shrimp into oil and fry until golden brown on each side. Mix hot sauce and melted butter together in a large bowl. Toss hot shrimp in sauce to coat. Serve with ranch dressing or dipping sauce of your choice. These are also fantastic on a bed of baby greens.

Sliced Flank Steak with Sweet Balsamic Glaze
Serves 4
Chef Bill likes this cut of beef because it's very lean and very tasty.

Ingredients:
1 1/2 to 2-pound flank steak
1 1/2 tablespoons smoked paprika
1 tablespoon sea salt
1/2 teaspoon ground pepper
1 teaspoon garlic powder
1 teaspoon onion powder
1/4 cup extra virgin olive oil

For the glaze:
2 shallots, very finely chopped
2 tablespoons small capers
2 tablespoons fresh thyme, finely chopped
3/4 cup good quality balsamic vinegar
1/4 cup quality sweetener such as honey, coconut palm nectar, or agave

Instructions: Use approximately 2 tablespoons of the olive oil to lightly coat steak. Whisk together all dry ingredients, then sprinkle, then pat seasoning mixture all over the steak. Refrigerate for at least three hours. Remove from refrigerator approximately 45 minutes prior to cooking. In a medium saute pan on medium heat, use remaining olive oil and sauté shallots until glassine, not browned. Add balsamic vinegar and whisk in sweetener until dissolved. Let simmer and reduce by approximately one-third. Add capers and thyme. Continue cooking and whisking for approximately 3 minutes. Cover and set aside.

Grill flank steak to desired doneness. For this recipe, rare is not recommended. Slice steak to desired thicknesses. Spoon warm glaze mixture over steak. (It may be necessary to reheat the glaze). Note: This glaze works well with any sort of beef - even meatballs!

Squishy Tuna on White Bread
Serves 1
When I want to go back to childhood, but don't want to go back to Wonder Bread, I do this:

Ingredients:
1 can tuna, drained
1/4 cup mayonnaise or veganaise
2 slices Udi's or Schar's GFwhite bread

Instructions:
In small mixing bowl, cream together tuna with mayo until tuna is almost paste-like. Because gluten-free bread is significantly stiffer than traditional white bread, spread a layer of mayo on each piece of bread, then add the tuna. Wrap tightly in Saran wrap or a plastic storage container and refrigerate overnight for maximum bread squishiness. If you can't wait that long...I understand.

A Walk On The Sweet Side

When we're having company for dinner and we're short on time, there's quite frankly, little that tops a chocolate cake made with a Namaste mix. It's so moist and spectacular, even friends and family who don't eat gluten-free ask for it. But for when I've got the time and feel like being an alchemist with these recipes.

The Reformed Elvis
Makes 6 muffins

Not everyone's a fan of Elvis Presley's music, but the man himself was undeniably intriguing. How could he not be with the velvety voice, uber-charisma that practically made him glow in the dark, and white-hot fascination of his fans which only seems to have grown stronger with each decade since his 1977 passing. And then there was The King's attraction to food. His alleged comfort food binges even seemed to rival mine in ferocity and scope. For that, he has earned my eternal astonishment, because not many of my eating buddies could keep up with me. I usually outperformed them all. I feel a twinge of sadness anytime I hear of a binge-eater (famous or not) who never escaped the cycle that goes something like this: gluttony, self-loathing, severe dieting... repeat. It's really quite awful. I was stuck in it for decades. But I was luckier than Elvis and his generation. I was bolstered by phenomenons such as the self-help movement, New Age spirituality, The Oprah Winfrey Show, pop psychology, and various factions of the fat acceptance army who, little by little, illumined to me the truth that I wasn't a horrible piece of crap after all... just a wounded one, who needed love and acceptance much more than she needed a diet or gym membership.

This book is living proof of the reformation of my eating habits and I knew that if were going to stick long-term, I'd have to make over most of my comfort foods. Like these banana "bread" muffins for instance! The word "bread" is qualified because there's no flour involved. They get their heft from Garbanzo beans and sweetness from bananas, but they taste and feel enough like banana bread to disseminate the recipe and let you be the judge. The Elvis part came after wondering aloud if this might possibly work as a clean version of one of the King's favorite snacks: the peanut butter and banana sandwich, which he preferred pan-fried if the legend is correct. In my own adventures with reformed eating, I've come to learn that it's enough to approximate flavors and textures of decadent concoctions such as the above sandwich. As long as I'm getting the genuine flavor and texture of bananas, bread, and peanut butter, I'm good. It doesn't have to be jammed between two slices of butter-smeared, squishy white bread and fried to a greasy crisp.

So here it is, my version of Elvis' beloved snack. And considering the brilliance of the pairing of peanut butter and banana, I have to say I agree with the King on this one. It's an irresistible combination. And would like to think that if Mr. Elvis Aaron Presley had access to all the help I did to get me where I am today, he just might try, if he were here today, one or two of these sweet and sticky little gems... and probably like them.

Ingredients:
1 can garbanzo beans, drained
2 eggs
2 bananas, nice and ripe (overripe's OK too)
1 teaspoon vanilla
1 tablespoon coconut oil
Preheat oven to 325. Blend all ingredients in a food processor until smooth. This will take a few minutes and require some scraping of the sides. Spray a six-muffin tin with cooking spray. (Or use a medium sized loaf pan). Place batter in each muffin cup, filling 1/2 to 3/4 of the way. Bake for 30 minutes then turn oven off and let muffins cool in the over another 15-20 minutes. Bean-based batters tend to be "wet" and heavy, so a little extra heat is required. Enjoy muffins at room temperature or

when still slightly warm. * Optional: Slather tops with peanut, almond, cashew, or sunflower seed butter. Proceed to moan.

Flourless Peanut Butter Cookies
Makes about 20 cookies
These treats are delicious and nutritious. You won't miss the flour!

Ingredients:
1 1/2 cups natural (non-hydrogenated) peanut butter
1/2 cup agave or coconut palm sugar
1 tablespoon vanilla
2 eggs, well beaten

Instructions:
Preheat oven to 350. In a mixing bowl, beat all ingredients with an electric hand mixer until smooth. Spray a large baking sheet generously, or line it with parchment paper. Scoop cookie dough into balls about the size of a ping-pong ball. Place onto baking sheet and flatten with the back of a fork, making a cross-cross pattern. Bake cookies for 10 minutes or until golden around the edges. Let cool for five minutes before transferring to a plate or rack. Enjoy with a glass of almond milk or cup of herbal tea.

Cherry-Coconut Cobbler
Serves 4
Emotional Eating Disclaimer:
With something this delicious, the fact that it's a 'clean' gluten and dairy-free recipe could delude the eater into believing eating half or perhaps the entire tray may not be such a bad idea (trust me, I've been there). So I corral my portions into small dishes like this pyrex glass dish (about 3/4 cup). So HANDY!

Ingredients:
Filling
1 22-ounce jar or can of cherry pie filling or the frozen berry equivalent

1/2 cup grapefruit juice
1 tablespoon lemon juice

Crust
2 1/2 cups water
1 cup cornmeal
2 teaspoons olive oil
1 teaspoon salt
1/4 cup sugar
2 teaspoons vanilla
1/2 cup coconut powder or unsweetened shredded coconut

Instructions:Preheat oven to 330. Spray an 8 x 10 baking pan with cooking spray and set aside. Bring water to a boil and add cornmeal, salt, sugar, vanilla, and oil and whisk vigorously. Reduce heat to low and continue whisking until mixture is thick. Turn heat off and whisk in coconut. The cornmeal should be porridge consistency but not runny. If too thick, add a bit of hot water. Pour fruit into baking pan. Drizzle the two juices over the fruit and mix slightly so it's evenly distributed. With a rubber spatula, drop cornmeal bit by bit on top of the fruit and spread slightly so it's an even crust. Bake for 35 minutes. Serve hot.

Mother Earth's Chocolate Mousse
Serves 1
Is there anyone who doesn't adore chocolate mousse? It's one of my all-time favorite out-to-dinner desserts because it's difficult to screw up. Even a mediocre restaurant tends to get it right. Probably because it's so simple: heavy cream, sugar and lots of chocolate. Who wouldn't love it? The only problem is... it doesn't love me. After eating a serving (or two) of the traditional version, I usually feel throat-coated and sluggish. During the dieting years, I recall a comically unsuccessful attempt to make chocolate mousse a part of a healthy eating plan via a rather, shall we say, marketing-savvy celebrity whose cottage empire of diet books centered around the declaration that all carbs are vile and fat is to be embraced. This product-hawking sweetie's diet plan was similar to Atkins,

only about 10 times more decadent. She even had a chocolate-mousse mix, made easily available by ordering off her website, or from the home shopping channel that helped her rake in millions. Do I sound annoyed at her? Well maybe a little. Let's just get real for a minute: anyone who knows anything about healthy eating, weight loss, or maintaining a healthy weight will probably agree with me when I say: STAY THE HECK AWAY FROM HEAVY CREAM! Have it in moderate amounts with coffee if you must. Or at least make it a semi-annual event, like the creamed pearl onions I love at Thanksgiving. Have you noticed that many restaurants are phasing it out of their cream soups and coming up with dessert alternatives that don't involve artery-clogging ingredients?

Yes, fat is your friend, but with one important caveat -- in order for it to be a friendship that's a two-way street, it has to be a plant-based fat. No one's gotten ill over a diet generous in olive, macadamia, coconut or sunflower oil. Ditto for nuts, and my all-time favorite: the avocado!

Unless you're in Santa Fe or Santa Monica, you probably won't find the avocado version of chocolate mousse in many restaurants, so go ahead and make it for yourself when you want something creamy, comforting and unmistakably chocolatey. It's both an elegant, dinner-party-worthy dessert and a tension diffuser. I have no trouble admitting that, steeped in the trappings of a frustrating deadline-ridden afternoon earlier today, this handy-dandy dessert is the only thing that kept me from screaming like a leading lady in a Hitchcock flick. Ingredient amounts are mutable -- adjust according to your preference for sweetness and chocolate-decibel level. This isn't low in fat, but I suggest you not fret about it. The mousse is loaded with monounsaturated fat, potassium, folate, pantothenic acid, vitamin E and several B vitamins. Heavy cream may be tasty, but doesn't even begin to touch the list of attributes that an avocado possesses.

This treat requires a little advanced planning. I prefer buying unripened avocados and letting them sit a few days. The taste is fresher than buying avocados in an already-soft state. When an avocado is ready for eating, its skin will give a little when

100

pressed, but shouldn't feel squishy. So here's to your health and the satisfaction of your sweet tooth -- with an all-natural treat that treats your body like royalty!

Ingredients:
1 ripe Hass avocado
1 teaspoon vanilla extract
8 drops of Stevia or one packet (or 1-2 tablespoons honey or agave. (I use Stevia because of its low glycemic index.)
2 tablespoons unsweetened baking cocoa or raw cacao powder*
A splash or two of espresso or strong coffee
* There's a second option for the chocolate flavoring: a wonderful chocolate powder my nutritionist, Nancy Guberti, turned me onto called Cocoa Mojo. It's a vegan, non-alkalized cocoa powder sweetened with organic coconut palm sugar and infused with immune system-supporting herbs. All I know is it tastes amazing. If you use two tablespoons of this instead of regular cocoa powder, skip the sweetener.

Instructions:
Peel and pit avocado and cut into large chunks. Place in a food processor along with the other ingredients and whir till smooth. You may need to add a tablespoon or two of coffee if it's too chunky. Scrap sides with scraper to make sure all the cocoa is evenly distributed. Whir some more until all the lumps are eradicated. Serve in something proper like a wine glass or dessert glass.

Mother Earth's Pistachio Pudding
Serves 1
She's done it again! The generous and bountiful Mother Nature divined another earth-originated dessert my way one afternoon when I was about to make chocolate mousse out of an avocado and noticed a bag of pistachios in the cupboard. The wheels started turning: the nuts are green...the avocado's green...this could work! And though I don't dwell on things like this...I sometimes miss the taste of pistachio desserts. So off to the food processor I skipped, and this is what I came up with:

Ingredients:
1 ripe Haas avocado
2-3 tablespoons shelled pistachios
1 teaspoon vanilla
8-10 drops Stevia or 1 tablespoon
coconut nectar or agave

Instructions:
Place nuts in food processor and
blend for a minute or two until
sandy and almost a paste. Cut
avocado in half and scoop out the
fruit into the food processor and
add vanilla and sweetener. Blend
until completely smooth. Scrape into dessert and garnish with a
few pistachios.

Banana "Ice Cream"

I'm always learning from my friend and mentor, Terri Lange.
She's also known as the Godmother of DDPYOGA and in the
nearly five years I've known her, she has generously imparted
countless tips and strategies that have helped me get my life
back, drop 185 pounds, and actually enjoy the ride. The 185
pounds are long gone, but being healthy and staying that way
doesn't have a finish line. And she's been an amazing example
of staying the course in the face of busy schedules, culinary
temptations, and plain old stress. Still, when Terri shared with
me one of her favorite tricks of the staying-svelte trade, I was
skeptical. Her go-to food when she craves ice cream? Frozen
bananas. I know. Sounds tremendously decadent, doesn't it?
So much so that I simply dismissed it as an overly zealous way
to avoid the perils of ice cream. If my alternative was frozen
bananas, I'd rather have nothing.

Terri and I are both dairy-free, and for a time, we both got
our frozen dessert needs met via pints and bars of 'ice cream'
made from almond or coconut milk. Tasted fantastic, but they
were loaded with sugar and still pretty caloric. When Terri

gushed to me one day that a few frozen bananas chopped and whirred for several minutes in a food processor sent her to the moon with pleasure, I was happy for her. But I had no desire to try something that sounded so boring. I tend to get irritated with products and recipes claim to closely mimic the taste and texture of something I love, only to have the rug pulled out from under me when push comes to shove. So I left that particular tip from Terri in the dust. Until one sweltering summer afternoon. Call it the effects of being crazy from the heat wave (s), but I've found myself fantasizing about walking up to the window of my neighborhood soft-serve and ordering a giant…oh, never mind. You get where I'm going. I was even starting to rationalize that I deserved it and the calories wouldn't count anyway because the northeast had been crippled for weeks by a barely tolerable and bizarrely prolonged mercury spike.

They were quite crafty, these invisible, whispering demons that beckoned me to the land of sugar cones capped with puffy white frozen vanilla cream. That's when I knew it was time to freeze a few bananas and give them and Terri's remedy a whirl in my food processor. That's really the only other key ingredient you'll need for this concoction. Some unsweetened cocoa powder if you're in need of a chocolate ice cream fix. That's it, no sugar, no cream, no emulsifiers, nothing but bananas.

Did I like it? Uh-uh…I LOVED it. Taste and texture of this dessert are superb. But I won't toy with you and say it's JUST like ice cream. It's close…but there's no throat coat. No cream means a cleaner, lighter taste. The absence of fat is noticeable in terms of how it sits in your stomach. There's no, 'gee, I've gotta rest and regroup now" feeling that comes from eating something densely caloric, but that's OK….it's an easy feeling to get used to.

Ingredients:
2 frozen bananas, cut into 1-inch chunks
splash of vanilla (optional)

Instructions:
Place half the banana pieces in a food processor. Pulse for several minutes, stopping every so often to scrape sides and distribute evenly. When thoroughly blended, add remaining bananas and repeat the process until the entire batch has pureed into a smooth mixture with a texture similar to soft ice cream or gelato. If desiring chocolate, add a tablespoon of unsweetened cocoa powder to banana mixture and puree thoroughly until evenly distributed. Since bananas and peanut butter pair beautifully, adding a tablespoon or two of natural peanut butter makes it a whole different dessert. Pour into two dessert dishes and eat immediately. May also be frozen in Tupperware and stored for up to a week.

Coconut Rice Pudding
Serves 6
This is a gluten-free, dairy-free dessert that knocks everyone's socks off. Doesn't matter how embedded they are in the world of pastries, cookies, or other forms of junk food, a bite of this rich, creamy dessert usually stops people in their tracks. It's vegan, but still rich and caloric, so it's a treat. My favorite time to eat a bowl is after a vigorous workout like Double Black Diamond, or a long power-walk. It's also fairly simple to make.
Ingredients:
2 cans coconut milk
1 cup white rice or Arborio rice (risotto)
1/2 teaspoon sea salt
1 teaspoon vanilla
1/4 cup coconut palm sugar or agave or 30 drops stevia

Instructions:
In a large non-stick saucepan, heat coconut milk to just simmering and add rice, salt, and vanilla. Turn heat back to medium low and simmer covered for about 20 minutes or until most of liquid has absorbed. Rice should be creamy and a little liquidy, not dry. Add sweetener and turn off heat and let stand covered for 10 minutes before serving. Keeps for up to a week refrigerated.

Quinoa Chocolate Cake
Makes a double-layer cake
This recipe was inspired by a quinoa chocolate cake recipe on the wonderful blog, "Making Thyme For Health." The photo looked so good I immediately rushed out to the store for a bag of white quinoa. This is hands down my favorite clean dessert. The coconut whipped cream frosting makes it irresistible. I find the flavor and texture of the whipped cream to be so divine, no sweetener is needed. If you disagree, feel free to add coconut palm sugar or Stevia. There are a few steps to this one, but it's worth the extra effort:

Ingredients:
For the cake:
2 cups cooked quinoa (not red)
1/3 cup unsweetened almond milk
4 eggs
1 teaspoon vanilla extract
1/2 cup coconut oil
1/4 cup melted coconut oil
1/2 cup coconut palm sugar
1 cup unsweetened cocoa powder or raw cacao powder
1/2 teaspoon baking soda
1 1/2 teaspoons baking powder
1/2 teaspoon salt

Whipped Chocolate Coconut Cream Frosting
2 (13.5 ounce) cans of full fat coconut milk, refrigerated

overnight
1/2 cup cocoa powder or raw cacao powder

Instructions:
Preheat the oven to 350°F and spray two cake pans with cooking spray. In a food processor or blender, combine the eggs, almond milk and vanilla and blend for ten seconds to combine. Add the quinoa along with the melted and cooled coconut oil and and the solid coconut oil, and blend until completely smooth, about thirty seconds to one minute. Sift together the dry ingredients in a large bowl. Add the wet ingredients in the food processor to the bowl with the dry and mix together until well combined. Divide the batter between the two pans and bake for 30 minutes. Remove the cakes from the oven and allow to cool.

For the frosting:
Remove the coconut milk from the refrigerator but don't shake the can or turn it upside down before opening. Open the can and scoop out the solid parts with a spoon, placing them in a medium sized mixing bowl. With an electric beater, beat on low speed for a minute until it starts to fluff. Carefully add the cocoa powder in increments so it doesn't scatter. Continue adding cocoa powder until it's thoroughly blended and frosting has a mocha color. Transfer first layer of the cake to a plate and begin frosting. When both layers are frosted, refrigerate cake for about 20 minutes before serving to set the frosting. Depending on the season, coconut cream frosting can 'wilt' in the heat. This cake stays refrigerated for up to two weeks if stored in an airtight manner. It also freezes well, in slices.

Coconut Whipped Cream
I credit Angela Liddon of the fantastic vegan "Oh She Glows" blog for this life-changing discovery. I was searching for a gluten-free version of Scottish shortbread for a Team DDPYOGA member and stumbled upon her site and couldn't stop reading her wonderful

recipes. This was one of them and it changed m life. I make this two cans at a time when I'm in the mood because it keeps in the refrigerator for more than a week. That way I can dip into it when I have a craving. It's a great topper to the bean cakes I make without frosting.

Instructions:
Refrigerate two cans of coconut milk overnight. When ready to make the cream, remove from refrigerator and turn the can upside down before opening. Let coconut water drain out and reserve for drinking straight or a as a smoothie base. Place coconut cream in a mixing bowl and blend on low, then medium speed until fluffy. That's it. This stuff is so good it doesn't even need sugar or vanilla!

Vanilla Cake with Chocolate Avocado Frosting
Makes 1 round layer cake
Another idea I got from Terri Lange, who introduced me to the art and practice of flour-free baking. I tend to craft most of my sweet treats out of bean-based cookies and cakes. It's lower in calories, higher in fiber, and leaves me feeling more balanced and satisfied. I got the avocado frosting after seeing how well it worked as a mousse, so why not frosting?

Ingredients:
1 can Garbanzo Beans, drained
2 eggs, room temperature
2 tablespoons coconut oil (note: it's normal for coconut oil to be solid at room temperature, except in warm-weather months)
25 drops of Stevia (or 1/3 cup agave, sugar, or coconut palm sugar or nectar)
1 teaspoon vanilla
1 teaspoon baking powder
1/4 teaspoon salt

Instructions:
Preheat oven to 350. Process all ingredients in a food processor until thoroughly blended and beans are liquified, scraping sides
107

of the food processor if necessary. The texture should be similar to pancake batter, perhaps a bit thicker. Coat a round cake pan with cooking spray thoroughly and pour batter into pan. Bake for 30 minutes before doing a toothpick. Continue to bake in five-minute increments as needed.

Frosting:
1 ripe Haas avocado
1 tablespoons Coco Mojo (see glossary)
2 tablespoons Raw Cacao Powder
1 teaspoon vanilla

Instructions:
Process all ingredients in a food processor. It may be necessary to add a few teaspoons of coffee or water to thin it out. Frost contents over the layer of cake and enjoy!

Pistachio Cake with Whipped Cream
Makes 1 round layer cake
Gloriously green...and good!

Ingredients:
1 can Great Northern Beans, drained
2 eggs, room temperature
2 tablespoons coconut oil (note: it's normal for coconut oil to be solid at room temperature, except in warm-weather months)
1 teaspoon vanilla
1 teaspoon baking powder
1/4 teaspoon salt
1 box sugar-free pistachio pudding

Instructions:
Preheat oven to 350 and spray a round cake pan with cooking spray. Blend all ingredients in a food processor thoroughly. The pudding mix may make the batter overly thick, if this happens, add a bit of water. Scrape into cake pan and bake for 25 minutes or until center feels firm to touch. Let cool, then cut into slices and top with coconut whipped cream (see recipe).

Fudgy Black Bean Brownies

Low heat is the secret to getting these brownies chewy and moist. These are a snack because they taste like a cookie jar item but are LOADED with nutrients!

Ingredients:
2 cups cooked black beans or canned no-salt added or low sodium black beans, drained
10 Medjool dates - pitted
2 tablespoons almond butter
1 teaspoon vanilla
1/2 cup natural, non-alkalized unsweetened cocoa powder
1/2 cup coconut palm sugar
1 tablespoon chia seeds
2 tablespoons unsweetened shredded coconut

Instructions:
Preheat oven to 200 degrees. Blend the black beans, dates, (double check for pits in the dates) almond butter and vanilla in a food processor or high-powered blender until smooth. Add the remaining ingredients and blend again. Pour into a very lightly oiled 8 x 8 inch baking pan and bake for 1 1/2 hours. Cool completely before cutting into small squares. Optional Topping:Blend 2 frozen bananas and a handful of walnuts in a high speed blender or food processor and then top off the brownies.

- Submitted by Terri Lange, Godmother of DDPYOGA

Homemade Candy Bars

Terri Lange shared this with me and it was begat from her DDPYOGA friend, Peggy, who begat the formula from Gwyneth Paltrow's recipe. I suspect the ingredients have changed a bit along the way, but here's the recipe as Terri presented it to me. These are DELICIOUS!

Ingredients:
1 1/2 cups raw cashews
1 1/2 cups pitted dates, chopped
1/2 cup almond butter
1/2 cup grade B maple syrup (or coconut palm nectar)
1/2 cup coconut flour
1/2 cup unsweetened shredded coconut
1/2 teaspoon almond extract
1 1/2 cups dark chocolate chips (60% or higher cocoa content or sugar-free chocolate chips)
1 1/2 tablespoons coconut oil

Instructions:
Grind the cashews to a very fine meal in a food processor. Add the dates, almond butter, maple syrup, coconut flour, shredded coconut and almond extract and then pulse until you have a sticky ball of dough. Line a small sheet/square/rectangle pan with parchment paper and press the cashew mixture out onto the paper, making a square/rectangle 1-inch deep. It helps if you put a drop of oil or water on your hands before doing this. Refrigerate the mixture for 6 to 8 hours, until it's firm.

Meanwhile, combine the chocolate chips and coconut oil in a double boiler (or use a stainless steel or glass bowl set over a pot of simmering water making sure the water doesn't touch the bowl). Stir the mixture until it's just melted, remove the bowl from the heat and pour the chocolate mixture over the cold cashew mixture. Return the bar mixture to the refrigerator and let it cool until the chocolate coating is set for at least 1 hour. Using the parchment, lift the bar out of the sheet pan and cut it into rectangles. You can use cookie cutters to make fun shapes for kids.

Glossary/Index

Gluten-free and dairy-free brands I love:
Namaste
Schar
Pamela's
1-2-3 Gluten-Free
Udi's breads
Trader Joe's, Silk, and Almond Breeze almond milk
Trader Joe's and So Delicious coconut milk
Coco Mojo - An all natural, coconut-palm-sugar sweetened cocoa that's great in recipes and in almond-milk-based hot chocolate. Bonus: it also contains dried, pulverized (meaning totally undetectable) mushrooms that boost the immune system.
Goya or Vitarroz canned coconut milk (for baking and making coconut whipped cream)
So Delicious Barista style creamer - For both coffee and as cream replacement in recipes
Tierra Farms Nuts and Nut Butters - Made with organic and fair trade ingredients, these clean and delicious nut butters are almost like dessert in a jar.

Equipment and gadgets that come in handy
A tagine is a round baking dish, North African in origin, with a fitted, cone-shaped lid. It's conical top conducts condensation and returns it to the bottom of the dish, imbuing its contents with a delicate gulf stream of steam. The result: falling-off-the-bone meat, velvety soft potatoes, or fragrant, juicy baked fruit.

Potato Masher - This wood-handled wonder is great not only for mashing potatoes (see recipe). It works well for blending ground meat and spices, IE, meatballs or meatloaf.

Nespresso Frothing Pitcher - Froths almond milk into a velvety brew better than any expensive cafe ever could. We use it every morning for almond milk latte's. Not cheap, but worth every dime.

Superfoods
Ever since reading Julie Morris' wonderful "Superfood

Kitchen" cookbook, I've been hooked on superfoods: berries, powders, and juices source largely from the Amazon rainforest and Andean mountains, which bear an unusually high nutrient and anti-oxidant content. I add them to smoothies, cakes, puddings, cookie bars, cereals...just about anything that's appropriate. Aside from the south American treasures, there are other nutrient-packed foods such as chia seeds, flax seeds, and coconut oil and I use them all regularly. My body has never felt so appreciated...or nourished!

Chia Seeds and Chia Seed Flour

Chia seeds are one of the most perfect foods in all of nature. There's debate on black va. white chia seeds and which one is healthier. They're both fantastic because they're both high in protein, fiber, and Omega 3 fatty acids, which means your hunger will be kept at bay. The mild, slightly nutty flavor of chia seeds makes them a natural for adding to hot cereal, in rice dishes, soups, puddings, and in drinks. Chia flour can be used in baking and is a great way to add nutrients and fiber to desserts. I cut the white flours called for in half and replace with chia flour. Chia seeds can be made into a fortifying drink by mixing two tablespoons with a glass of water, stirring vigorously, and drinking after about 10 minutes, by which time the mixture will be gel-like and thick. And I LOVE adding a few tablespoons of chia flour to a protein drink to turn if fluffy and thick.

Hemp Hearts

I was skeptical when I first laid eyes on these greenish little seeds. They didn't look overly appetizing but after trying some in a smoothie, I was astonished to discover they quelled my hunger for hours afterward. And they have a mild, nutty flavor. Three tablespoons is all you need and here's what you get: 170 calories, 10 g. of polyunsaturated fat, 10 g of protein, iron, riboflavin, phosphorus, magnesium, zinc, and 110 percent daily value of manganese. I also love them on salads and in avocado pudding. SO fortifying!

Flax Seeds

Remember wheat germ? My dad used to sprinkle it on his

cold cereal for extra fiber and vitamins. Ground chia seeds and ground flax seeds are the wheat-free answer! Sometimes I even throw a few tablespoons in a smoothie.
Avocados

Coconut Oil

If I appear to be showing favoritism with the following soliloquy on coconut oil it's only because, well, it IS my favorite oil. I use it in smoothies, chocolate cakes, energy bars, soups, and also on my skin - it's a fantastic moisturizer! Coconut oil is also a delicious baking companion for cooking poultry — rub some onto the skin prior to baking, then sprinkle with spice mixtures, such as curry powder, sage, or garlic. Coconut oil is also a good dip for boneless chicken breasts before coating them with breadcrumbs for baking or frying. And my new, favorite way to enjoy coconut oil - melted onto hot pancakes instead of butter...a valuable tip passed on from my genius nutritionist Nancy Guberti. I was skeptical at first, but it's absolutely delicious. Anyone remember the 80's and the bad rap that coconut oil got? Those studies were done using partially hydrogenated coconut oil while today's evidence is based on virgin, unprocessed, untreated coconut oil. The unhealthy part appears to be the hydrogenation process, which produces heart-damaging trans fats and also destroys essential fatty acids and needed antioxidants. Virgin coconut oil does contain saturated fats. However, its main saturated fat is lauric acid, a so-called medium-chain fatty acid, which, apparently, is more quickly metabolized and is less likely to leave fat deposits in our bodies.

There are other benefits. Studies suggest that foods rich in MCFAs can help burn calories; other findings show that lauric acid can help boost the immune system, and still others offer some evidence that the properties in virgin coconut oil can slow down the effects of Alzheimer's disease. The saturated fat in virgin coconut oil does not seem to change the ratio of HDL (high density lipoproteins: good cholesterol) to LDL (low density lipoprotein: bad cholesterol).

Cooking Oils

113

When cooking, and especially frying, with oil, it's important to choose one with a high flash point, meaning, it's able to take a significant amount of heat without smoking. Richly colored oils such as extra virgin olive oil and flax seed oil are great for salads and dipping, but not meant for cooking. Years ago, experiencing smoke inhalation while sautéing with extra virgin olive oil was my first clue that something was amiss. When oils smokes, it becomes carcinogenic, which defeats the purpose of assembling a kitchen full of clean and healthy ingredients.

Oils with high smoking points - Excellent for sautéing and frying
Light olive oil, grapeseed oil, sunflower seed oil, sesame oil, avocado oil, coconut oil, and many of the nut oils such as peanut, macadamia, and hazelnut oils.

Oils with a low smoking point - Best for salads, bean dips, and dipping bread
Flax seed oil, extra virgin olive oil

<u>Ayurveda</u>
Deepak Chopra's 'Perfect Weight' and determining my dosha type was part of the mosaic I put in place back in the mid 90's, about 13 years before finding my fitness guru and being the ready student to put it all in place. There was plenty of sound advice in 'Perfect Weight' and I recommend it highly. And also, taking Chopra's dosha test. It will both answer questions about your constitution and give some valuable instructions for your particular type that you can put in place immediately: (http:// doshaquiz.chopra.com).

15705820R00067

Made in the USA
San Bernardino, CA
03 October 2014